THE THREAT TO REASON

THE THREAT TO REASON

How the Enlightenment was hijacked
and how we can reclaim it

DAN HIND

VERSO

London • New York

First published by Verso 2007
© Dan Hind 2007
All rights reserved

1 3 5 7 9 10 8 6 4 2

Verso
UK: 6 Meard Street, London W1F 0EG
USA: 180 Varick Street, New York, NY 10014-4606
www.versobooks.com

Verso is the imprint of New Left Books

ISBN-13: 978-1-84467-152-6

British Library Cataloguing in Publication Data
A catalogue record for this book is available from the British Library

Library of Congress Cataloging-in-Publication Data
A catalog record for this book is available from the Library of Congress

Typeset in Bembo by Hewer Text UK Ltd, Edinburgh
Printed and bound in the USA by Quebecor World

For Geoffrey and Diana
With my love.

Contents

Introduction

Why Enlightenment? Why Now?

Mark you this, you proud men of action, you are nothing but the unconscious henchmen of intellectuals, who, often in the humblest seclusion, have meticulously plotted your every deed.
Heinrich Heine, *History of Religion and Philosophy in Germany*, Vol. III (1834)

When the famously religiose President Bush visited Britain less than a year after the invasion of Iraq, he traced the Anglo-American alliance to a shared history. Prominent in this shared history were the great secular figures of the eighteenth-century British Enlightenment:

> We're sometimes faulted for a naive faith that liberty can change the world. If that's an error it began with reading too much John Locke and Adam Smith.[1]

This might surprise those who think that Bush's desire to bring liberty to the world derives from his homespun Evangelical Christianity. But it becomes more comprehensible when we see how the language and the great figures of the Enlightenment have always run alongside religious rhetoric in his and earlier American administrations.

In a speech on the third anniversary of the US–UK invasion of Iraq, Prime Minister Blair claimed that Europe's history of 'renaissance, reformation and enlightenment' had left the Muslim and

Arab world 'uncertain, insecure and on the defensive'. While some in the Middle East had responded to the challenge of modernity with a secular project of their own, he said, others had retreated into the consolations of unreason, seeking salvation in a 'combination of religious extremism and populist politics':

> It is the age-old battle between progress and reaction, between those who embrace and see opportunity in the modern world and those who reject its existence; between optimism and hope on the one hand; and pessimism and fear on the other.

Blair did not simply identify progress and modernity with the West. He acknowledged that Hindus, Christians, Jews and Muslims could all 'believe in religious tolerance, openness to others, to democracy, liberty and human rights administered by secular courts'[2]. Yet still, those who oppose Anglo-American policies in the Middle East are the enemies of modernity. Worship anyone you like, Blair seems to be saying, as long as you believe in the existence of the Anglo-American 'War on Terror'.

In one way or another, the Enlightenment regularly appears in attempts to explain and justify the high politics of our times. Elite groups in the West gain self-confidence and solidarity from the idea that they are the guardians of the Enlightenment. After all, in the words of Victor Davis Hanson, the Enlightenment 'established the western blueprint for a humane and ordered civilization'[3]. Neo-conservatives energetically try to associate themselves with progress and the spread of enlightened modernity.[4] Neoliberals draw on the authority of the eighteenth-century liberals to justify their economic theories about the need to replace state handouts with private initiative; according to Milton Friedman, perhaps the most influential economist of the second half of the twentieth century, the *Wall Street Journal* 'has repeatedly stressed its view that the invisible hand of Adam Smith is a far more effective and equitable means of organizing economic activity than the visible hand of government'[5]. *The Economist* proudly declares its allegiance to free-market liberalism and takes every opportunity to secure the spectral support of the eighteenth-century Scottish political economist Adam Smith for its editorial line, often in the most exotic contexts:

> Rachel Carson, the crusading journalist who inspired greens in the 1950s and 60s, is joining hands with Adam Smith, the hero of free-marketeers. The world may yet leapfrog from the dark ages of clumsy, costly, command-and-control regulations to an enlightened age of informed, innovative, incentive-based greenery.[6]

Rachel Carson, for many the founder of the modern environmental movement, is safely dead and cannot tell us what she thinks about incentive-based greenery. Adam Smith can say nothing about the constant invocation of his name to justify modern policies, or the suggestion that somewhere, for some reason, he is holding hands with Rachel Carson.

Meanwhile, many of our intellectuals and serious journalists are preoccupied with the threat to the Enlightenment posed by its irrational enemies. According to the conventional wisdom, the Enlightenment is permanently in danger, requiring constant protection against the forces of unreason. 'The new Rome that science built is under siege by the barbarians',[7] declares the avowedly enlightened British politician Dick Taverne. The *New Scientist* worries that, 'after two centuries in the ascendancy, the Enlightenment project is under threat. Religious movements are sweeping the globe preaching unreason, intolerance and dogma, and challenging the idea that rational, secular enquiry is the best way to understand the world'[8]. The American scholar Stephen Bronner argues that the conflict between the Enlightenment and its irrational enemies constitutes 'the great divide' of modern politics.

Powerful institutions and individuals in Britain and America seek to establish their legitimacy by claiming for themselves the enlightened inheritance. Politicians and the representatives of large companies alike insist that their policies are the product of disinterested reason and scientific inquiry. We can trust them to exercise great and often unaccountable power because they are imbued with the values of the Enlightenment. Their control of the concept of Enlightenment both expresses and secures their dominant position in the current political and economic system.

At the same time these powerful institutions and individuals readily compare their opponents with the forces of the Counter-Enlightenment, the ultra-conservatives who sought to defend traditional, hierarchical society from the levelling ambitions of the enlightened apostles of freedom in the eighteenth century. But even as they denounce their opponents' irrationality and intellectual immaturity and insist noisily on the need for open debate, they ignore or distort the arguments against them. None of those who fight the British and the Americans are resisting a foreign occupation, we are told, they are all seeking to stop progress, to enslave women, and to return Iraq and Afghanistan to the Dark Ages. Moreover, the millions who marched against the invasion of Iraq in 2003 did not seek to prevent an aggressive war, but to deny fundamental human rights to the people of the Middle East and 'to oppose the overthrow of a fascist dictator'[9]. In this way the invocation of the Enlightenment decays into a kind of blackmail – 'either you are for us, or you are against the progress and reason'[10].

This blackmailing use of the Enlightenment recurs constantly in our culture in attempts to marginalize resistance to unaccountable power. Apologists for corporate power complain that an anti-science mood is hindering technological advances in agriculture and industry; moves to regulate business stem from an irrational desire for a risk-free society; concerns about the economic and political structure of healthcare demonstrate how a rising tide of New Age unreason threatens to engulf us; opposition to the European Constitution was caused by an irrational fear of foreigners. In what follows I try to make this blackmail more difficult by separating the history and the potential of the historical Enlightenment from the uses made of it by established economic, political and cultural power. There is a great urgency in this, since the drive towards an ever more militarized and predatory world system relies heavily, perhaps finally depends on, the continued effectiveness of this blackmail.

This, then, is what this book seeks to describe and to challenge – the threat to reason posed by allegedly enlightened institutions, above all by the state and the corporation. The threat these institutions pose to rational inquiry is largely missing from recent attempts to defend the Enlightenment. These, as we shall see, focus instead on the enemies of the enlightened inheritance that sportingly identify themselves as such: fundamentalist Christians, New Age mystics and postmodern academics, for example. In these accounts the Enlightenment faces off against its enemies in a confrontation that has all the stereotypical clarity of a wrestling match, and all the explanatory merit of an exploitation film. This confrontation all but monopolizes our sense of what it would mean to be enlightened today. Its impresarios and promoters insist they are being drowned out by their irrational enemies, even as they saturate broadcasting and journalism. They demand that we face reality while concocting ever more unlikely coalitions of the Old Testament and the New Age. They denounce the credulity of the public, while peddling ever more absurd fantasies. As much as anything, it is this mini-genre of lip-smacking cultural and political misdirection that has prompted the writing of this book.

I don't propose to present a detailed account of what the Enlightenment was in historical terms. Rather I want to test the plausibility and usefulness of certain contemporary uses of the concept. Further to that, I want to show how the institutions that claim collectively to embody the Enlightenment, above all the state and the corporation, pose the most serious threat to a reasoned understanding of our times. It is a threat that is all the more serious for being hidden beneath a rhetorical commitment to open debate and free inquiry.

Still, when I refer to the historical Enlightenment I am referring to a more or less self-conscious and unified movement in Europe and North America in the seventeenth and eighteenth centuries that rejected established authority as the basis for knowledge and insisted that only experience could provide us with reliable information about the world. Following the advice of pioneering scientific legislator Francis Bacon, the philosophers of the Enlightenment tried to rid themselves of the elaborate systems that passed for knowledge and to discover for themselves all they could about the world, including the limits of knowledge. It is a desire to establish sure foundations for knowledge, a preoccupation with discovering the truth, that characterize the great figures of the Age of Enlightenment.

My concern is to examine how ideas from the historical Enlightenment function in contemporary society. Politicians and intellectuals most often define the Enlightenment in terms of its opposition to the forces of unreason, whether they be *jihadis*, fascists or homeopaths; this I shall refer to as the 'Folk Enlightenment', so called because the tune will be familiar to most readers, even if the lyrics change somewhat as the context demands. I will also later introduce the terms 'Occult Enlightenment' and 'Open Enlightenment' to distinguish between two very different successors to the historical Enlightenment: the state's secret quest for total knowledge under conditions of perfect secrecy, and a more faltering, but wholly human, attempt to achieve a more universal understanding and so to make another world possible.

Some people will object to this, and point out how much of the concept of Enlightenment this account leaves out, and how much is smuggled into it. And they are right, of course. From some perspectives the Enlightenment looks like the final development in the history of the Protestant Reformation, and the separation of church and state in North America seems to be its culminating triumph. Conservatives in the past have argued that the Enlightenment was above all a matter of cultish obsession with reason and progress that ended in the utopian terror of the French Revolution. Jonathan Israel, a man who knows as much about the history of the Enlightenment as any man alive, contrasts the radical Enlightenment of Baruch Spinoza, the great Jewish scholar and religious sceptic, with the temporizing and limited Enlightenment of Locke and Voltaire. Those, like Peter Gay, who are more favourable to the French Enlightenment, see Voltaire by contrast as a, perhaps the, central representative figure. Postmodernists from Theodor Adorno onwards have pointed out how the Enlightenment's campaign to understand the world coincided with a murderous European attempt to conquer it. But the Enlightenment wasn't a single historical event like the Louisiana Purchase or the fall of Constantinople; it was a composite of overlapping and sometimes contradictory impulses. Besides, for our purposes, what it was is less important than what it might be. That is, our concern is to establish what we learn from the history of the seventeenth and eighteenth centuries.

In Chapter 1 I try to show how particular ideas about the Enlightenment have operated in recent political, cultural and economic debates. My aim is to explore in greater detail the idea that a neat binary division can be made between Enlightenment and its enemies – a 'great divide'. This is an idea that saturates our intellectual culture. Increasingly it also helps to justify the conditions of emergency in which we find ourselves. Since 9/11 vigorous attempts have been made to identify Western states with the enlightened inheritance and to persuade us that these values face extinction at the hands of an entirely alien and irrational enemy. A bare handful of terrorist renegades re-enacts the totalitarian assault on reason defeated in the Second World War. Once we have considered how the idea of Enlightenment functions in contemporary debate, in Chapter 2 I look quickly at the historical Enlightenment of the seventeenth and eighteenth centuries. This doesn't pretend to be a history of the Enlightenment. It is more like grave-robbing than respectable archaeology.

In Chapters 3 to 6 I look again at the dominant modern understanding of what it means to be enlightened, at the various versions of the Folk Enlightenment. The aim here is to take seriously the suggestion made by many intellectuals and commentators that the Enlightenment can be understood adequately as a secular, liberal modernity threatened by irrational, extremist or totalitarian enemies. So I take a little time to consider the alleged 'threat to reason' posed by fundamentalist religion, postmodernism and New Age opponents of science. In Chapter 7 I describe what seems to me to be more serious threats to reason and truth, enemies that would have frightened and outraged Voltaire.

Finally, in Chapter 8, I go back to the writings of the European Enlightenment and see what, if anything, it can offer us in terms of practical advice. Once we have cleared away some of the mummery and cant that surrounds the work of the great founding philosophers of modernity, we will find, I think, that it is possible to rediscover an aggressive, world-changing Enlightenment. This Enlightenment, far from needing protection, finds expression in an attack on the mythical consolations offered to us by the prevailing culture, including those that draw on a bowdlerized and historically disembodied Enlightenment. Enlightenment understood in this way must resemble its historical predecessor in one respect: it will savage much that passes for knowledge at the present time.

Once we begin to think of Enlightenment in these terms, politicians will find it more difficult to invoke the glories of Western civilization to justify their actions, and intellectuals, who at present find in the Enlightenment a safe way to seem daring, will run an increased risk of appearing ridiculous. So the book has two aims, one destructive, one constructive. Firstly, I want to destroy the persuasiveness of the idea that the Enlightenment is something that must be defended against its irrational enemies, as though it were an invalid or a helpless child. Secondly, I want to establish a more convincing account of what it would mean to be enlightened right now. Friedrich Nietzsche, himself a ferocious critic of the Enlightenment, once said that one should philosophize with a hammer.[11] I want to take a hammer to that faintly numinous word 'Enlightenment'. But I want us to make a hammer from the philosophy and history of the Enlightenment.

London, February 2007

1

The Party of Modernity

The Enlightenment has always been central to political debate in the modern West. Karl Marx drew on and sought to transcend the Enlightenment in his work. The struggle between totalitarian movements and their opponents in the mid-twentieth century drew on the ideas of both the Enlightenment and its ideological enemies. During the era of post-war reconstruction, the Enlightenment provided political and cultural elites with a model of civilization, with an idea of Europe, untainted by the horrors of Nazism. Both sides in the Cold War sought to claim its legacy for themselves. In recent years we have seen the idea of Enlightenment and related concepts deployed extensively in two key elite projects: neoliberal globalization and the War on Terror. The first of these has declined somewhat in importance, but the War on Terror remains central to contemporary politics.

ADAM SMITH GOES GLOBAL

The ideas of economists and political philosophers, both when they are right and when they are wrong, are more powerful than is commonly understood. Indeed the world is ruled by little else. Practical men, who believe themselves to be quite exempt from any intellectual influences, are usually the slaves of some defunct economist.

John Maynard Keynes, *The General Theory of Employment, Interest and Money* (1936)

In Britain and America today's advocates of the free-market economy look to the seventeenth and eighteenth centuries for inspiration
and justification for their favoured policies.[1] The intellectual origins
of this modern interest in the British Enlightenment are complex.
Influential figures in the mid-twentieth century such as the Austrian
philosophers Friedrich Hayek and Karl Popper saw in eighteenth-
century liberalism the only realistic alternative to serfdom. The
presumption in favour of a small state and of economic freedom that
they saw in the work of Adam Smith and others suggested a politics
that would allow individuals to grow in moral and material stature.
Renovating and applying the principles of their version of the British
Enlightenment would provide a necessary counterweight to the
collectivizing impulses of the democratic and regulatory state. The
New Deal in America and the post-war welfare state in Britain
threatened, they thought, to bring about a more insidious version of
the totalitarianism that had engulfed much of Europe in the 1930s
and 1940s. The struggle to limit and even to roll back the regulatory
state was, they believed, nothing less than a struggle to defend the
enlightened ideal of freedom.

In 1938 Friedrich Hayek set up the Society for the Renovation of
Liberalism. Its members included the American columnist and early
theorist of modern public relations Walter Lippman, as well as Karl
Popper and Sir John Clapham, a Bank of England official who
would later head the Royal Society, Britain's most prestigious
scientific institution. Two years after the war, Hayek set up the
Mont Pelerin Society, which resumed the work of the earlier
group. Its members went on to create a large and influential
network of free-market think tanks that today include the Institute
for Economic Affairs and the Adam Smith Institute in Britain, and
the Heritage Foundation in the United States. In this way a
renovated liberalism – 'neoliberalism' – brought the ideas of the
eighteenth century into the mainstream of political agitation and
debate. Or, in more polemical terms, the prestige of the British
Enlightenment was used to prettify calls to reconstruct the econo-
mies of Britain, the United States and elsewhere, on terms more
favourable to the investing classes.

Neoliberals sought to remove the state from active involvement in the economy. Domestically they advocated privatization and deregulation in the private sector, reductions in welfare, and restrictions on collective bargaining. Internationally they supported free trade and the removal of controls on the movement of capital. As far as possible, they wanted to leave individuals free to make their own economic decisions; in this way, they reasoned, individuals would become more responsible for their circumstances. A properly moral economy would be restored in which prudence and thrift were rewarded and laziness was punished. Only in this way could Anglo-American society be reinvigorated.

These advocates of liberty found a receptive audience in Ronald Reagan and Margaret Thatcher, who helped to make important changes to the political economy of their countries. The language of free markets and invocations of the Enlightenment added intellectual lustre and a sense of public-spiritedness to assaults on the power of labour unions during the 1980s and the redistribution of wealth to the rich. But while intellectuals sought to resuscitate their nations through the application of the principles of the British Enlightenment, their allies in business and politics had more mixed motives. The political classes stopped well short of creating anything like genuinely free markets; strategic subsidies and other barriers to trade remained intact and the state continued to be a decisive actor in the private economy. The large corporations that supported neoliberal think tanks happily collaborated with fascist dictatorships in Latin America. Indeed corporate capitalism, neoliberal theorists, and fascist death squads managed something like a condominium in Chile in the years after 1971.[2]

Despite the very limited and only ambiguously liberal application of free-market policies in Britain, America and Chile, the collapse of the Soviet Union in 1991 greatly emboldened the neoliberal Right and allowed it to dream of one world united under free trade and the rule of law. Neoliberals were sure that they had discovered the secret of successful economic management. As part of their campaign to bring prosperity to the world they sought to associate enlightened ideas of progress and emancipation with the policy prescriptions associated with the World Bank and the International Monetary Fund. Here in the global institutions, enlightened experts could devise policies away from what they considered to be a fearful and ill-informed public.

Throughout the 1990s, politicians insisted that the market was putting new limits on what citizens could expect from their employers and from the state. There would have to be less regulation, especially of financial markets; labour would have to become more 'flexible' (i.e. workers would have to make do with less job security); tax policies would have to 'provide incentives for growth in order to attract enterprise and to maximize innovation and entrepreneurship'.[3] These were exciting times. The public would be freed from the dead hand of Big Government and raised up by Adam Smith's hidden hand. Instead of command and control, billions of individual decisions in a free and fair marketplace would determine the allocation of goods.[4] Voltaire's verdict on the capitalism of his time captures some of the idealism and excitement of neoliberal intellectuals in the period directly after the end of the Cold War:

> Go into the London Stock Exchange – a more respectable a place than many a court – and you will see representatives of all nations gathered there for the service of mankind. There the Jew, the Mohammedan, and the Christian deal with each other as if they were of the same religion, and give the name of infidel only to those who go bankrupt. There the Presbyterian trusts the Anabaptist, and the Anglican accepts the Quaker's promise.[5]

But it was Adam Smith who featured most prominently in the triumph of the free-market ideal in the late 1980s and early 1990s. His satisfyingly difficult and extensive works, combined with a little selective quotation, had long made Smith an idol for certain sections of the Right. In Britain the Adam Smith Institute has been a 'leading innovator of free-market economic and social policy'[6] since 1977. Famously, in what one imagines was a homage to the master, the free marketeers at the institute once proposed moving the population of Hong Kong to the Western Isles of Scotland to save them from the tyranny of Beijing, which is nothing if not in-novative.[7]

In the early 1990s with the fall of the USSR Adam Smith could at last go to Moscow[8] and his self-appointed heirs had a chance to realize his vision in full. In 1992 at the Adam Smith address to the National Association of Business Economists in the United States, the Prime Minister of Czechoslovakia, Vaclav Klaus, declared that he was 'convinced that Adam Smith supplies us with a vision of where to go that needs no correction'.[9] In the same year Boris Yeltsin's acting Prime Minister, Yegor Gaidar, was removing price controls and exposing the Russian economy to the free play of market forces. Gaidar later referred to Adam Smith's work as 'the basis of understanding the role of the market in private property and in economic development'.[10] After decades of often inept and almost always unaccountable state planning, the intelligentsia of the former Eastern Bloc believed that the eighteenth-century liberals showed the way to a better future. Compared with hollow platitudes about proletarian fraternity, Smith must have had the uncompromising ring of absolute truth:

> It is not from the benevolence of the butcher, the brewer, or the baker, that we expect our dinner, but from their regard to their own interest. We address ourselves, not to their humanity but to their self-love, and never talk to them of our necessities but of their advantages.[11]

Western governments and their allies in academia energetically promoted the idea that rapid, even disorderly, transition in Central and Eastern Europe was preferable to stagnation and the danger of a return to communism. Let markets work their magic immediately and everything else would follow.

The political and economic failure of the Soviet Union also encouraged the Left in Western Europe and North America to revive progressive traditions that pre-dated Marx. Ideas associated with the Enlightenment became much more likely to attract interest and adherents, especially among those who had never been attracted by the glamour of revolutionary communism and who doubted that Marxism had superseded the ideas of the Enlightenment. Marx himself was read in a different light, as an Enlightenment figure, a brilliant journalist and pioneering social scientist rather than the prophet of the historical necessity of the Gulag. A revived Left described a genealogy of Enlightenment that connected the traditions of eighteenth-century liberalism to the anarchist opponents of both Leninist Marxism and capitalism. Noam Chomsky made the link between the Enlightenment tradition and contemporary resistance to capitalism quite explicit. Asked what he meant by the claim that the classical liberals were anti-capitalists he explained:

> Well, the underlying, fundamental principles of Adam Smith and other classical liberals were that people should be free; they shouldn't be subjected to things like division of labor, which destroys them. So look at Smith: why was he in favor of markets? He gave kind of a complicated argument for them, but at the core of it was the idea that if you had perfect liberty, markets would lead to perfect equality – that's why Adam Smith was in favor of markets. Adam Smith was in favor of markets because he thought that people's fundamental character involves notions like sympathy, and solidarity, the right to control their own work, and so on and so forth: all the exact opposite of capitalism . . . Now the sources of power and authority that people could see in front of their eyes in the eighteenth century were quite different from the ones we have today – back then it was the feudal system, and the Church, and the absolutist state that they were focused on; they couldn't see the industrial corporation, because it didn't exist yet. But if you take the basic classical liberal principles and apply them to the modern period, then I think you actually come pretty close to the principles that animated revolutionary Barcelona in the late 1930s – to what's called 'anarcho-syndicalism'.[12]

The conflict between the global justice movement and the neo-liberals was perhaps the most important ideological event of the decade after the Cold War. To some considerable degree it turned on the legitimacy of neoliberal and anarchist claims to the Enlightenment heritage. In this debate it is only fair to say that the facts favoured the anarchists. Adam Smith strongly objected to the limited liability for investors. He believed that investors who stood to lose only their original stake would become reckless and negligent. Smith himself could therefore be enlisted by campaigners against corporate power.[13] The idea that corporations should enjoy the same human rights as people could find no support in classical liberalism. Indeed, those who supported the corporation-as-person had radically departed from the principles of the British Enlightenment. Classical liberalism had been greatly concerned about the rights of the individual, but never extended this concern to commercial institutions.

And among milder critics of corporate capitalism, quotation from Adam Smith could also serve a polemical purpose. The rejection of the neoliberal orthodoxy would often be accompanied by an insistence that the message of the founding father of economics had been distorted by over-zealous, even heretical, disciples at the IMF and the World Bank.[14] Pitted against the Adam Smith who talked of man's 'propensity to truck, barter and exchange one thing for another'[15] was the clear-eyed observer of commercial perfidy:

> People of the same trade seldom meet together, even for merriment and diversion, but the conversation ends in a conspiracy against the public, or in some contrivance to raise prices.[16]

With a little work, Adam Smith could be presented as an advocate of the regulatory state and of legislation to prevent unfair collusion between companies.

On the fringes of the struggle between the global justice protestors and the free-trade intelligentsia, among British academics the Enlightenment also featured prominently. 'Globalization' was important, so it had to have something to do with the Enlightenment.

The British academic John Gray identified free markets with the Enlightenment, and decisively rejected both.[17] On the other hand, Anthony Giddens accepted the inevitability of globalization but imagined that it marked the end of 'the dream of the Enlightenment philosophers',[18] arguing that the complexities of a global marketplace defied attempts at rational administration.[19] These mutually inconsistent models of Enlightenment were not greatly influential at the time and have more or less fallen away in the period after 2001. But they are worth noticing, insofar as they show how much, and how much that is contradictory, could be referred to by the word 'Enlightenment' in the period of 'globalization'.

The collapse of neoliberalism as an intellectually defensible project had become increasingly apparent by the turn of the century. Aggregate global growth in the 1990s stood at 1.1 per cent, compared with 3.5 per cent in the 1960s and 2.4 per cent in the 1970s, the era of stagflation.[20] In the developing world, low growth and recession had accompanied obedience to the Washington institutions' free-trade agenda:

> During the 1990s, Russian per capita income declined at the rate of 3.5 per cent annually. A large proportion of the population fell into poverty, and male life expectancy declined by five years as a result. Ukraine's experience was similar. Only Poland, which flouted IMF advice, showed any marked improvement. In much of Latin America neoliberalization produced either stagnation . . . or spurts of growth followed by economic collapse (as in Argentina).[21]

Perhaps the spectral support of Voltaire and Adam Smith helped the experts at the IMF and the World Bank to avoid looking too closely at the consequences of their policies; it certainly lent them a degree of prestige among non-experts. To criticize the Washington Consensus was to line up with the forces of reaction against the enlightened struggle for a better world. The impact on the real economy, and on those less familiar with the glories of eighteenth-century Edinburgh, was not always so agreeable. But the architects of rapid transformation in the former Eastern Bloc and the developing world, and their supporters in the media, remained confident of their enlightened credentials long after it had become apparent that they had presided over a series of terrible catastrophes.

China famously ignored the IMF and the World Bank and grew rapidly in the 1990s. Elsewhere in Asia, obedience to neoliberal orthodoxy correlated closely with financial crisis and severe recession in 1997 and 1998. Thailand, Indonesia, Malaysia and the Philippines liberalized their capital markets and suffered far more than those countries that had maintained exchange controls.[22]

In fact, neoliberalism, with its bracing talk of freedom and its appeals to the glories of British free-trade liberalism, had provided cover for a massive transfer of wealth to the rich. The top 0.1 per cent of income earners in the US tripled their share of national income to 6 per cent in the years between 1978 and 1999. In Britain the top 1 per cent doubled their share of national income in the two decades after 1982.[23] But neoliberalism had failed to restore growth rates to anything like the levels seen in the era of heavy regulation, nationalization and exchange controls. Its claim to the Enlightenment tradition, always shaky, was starting to look absurd. The world's rulers needed another story and they needed it fast.

THE PARTY OF MODERNITY

Remember the antitrade demonstrators? They were the top item in the news before terrorists attacked the World Trade Center. Now they have receded to the netherworld where we have tucked all the things that seemed important then.

Wall Street Journal editorial,
'Adieu Seattle?', 24 September 2001

The terrorist attacks on New York and Washington did much to obscure the history of the preceding decade. The idea that the enlightened inheritance was under attack from irrational enemies had received sudden, spectacular confirmation; the defenders of the established order could once again consider themselves enlightened.

There was an air of relief among advocates of neoliberal, corporate-friendly globalization that the accumulating evidence of intellectual bankruptcy suddenly belonged to a previous era, to the years before everything changed. Now they could forget the indignities of Seattle and Genoa, declare the debate about globalization over, and call on their opponents to unite against a common enemy. The then editor of the *New Republic*, Peter Beinart, called for the anti-globalization movement to recognize the new, wartime conditions:

> The anti-globalization movement is, in part, a movement mo-tivated by hatred of the global inequities between rich and poor. And it is, in part, a movement motivated by hatred of the United States. Now after what has happened this week it must choose . . . This nation is now at war. And in such an environment, political dissent is immoral without a prior statement of national solidarity, a choosing of sides.[24]

In this process of rapid intellectual readjustment, the Enlightenment once again featured very prominently. Writing in 2003, the histor-ian Darrin McMahon noted how, in the period directly after the attacks on the USA:

> One word kept coming up: 'Enlightenment'. 'Wanted, an Islamic Enlightenment to End Religious Intolerance', declared the headline of a Thomas Friedman column in the *International Herald Tribune* on December 16th, 2001. In the same week, the editors at the conservative *National Review* expressed regret that Islam had failed to undergo the 'chastening experience' of an Enlightenment (to say nothing of a Reformation or Counter-Reformation).[25]

The enlightened West had been attacked by enemies that were by definition quite irrational, so there was no need to seek an explanation for what had happened. Steve Weber, the Director of the Institute of International Studies at the University of California, Berkeley, noticed that the repeated references to the

Enlightenment in the period after 9/11 had the paradoxical effect of steering the public away from serious inquiry into the political context of the attacks:

> On September 12, the shelves were emptied of books on Islam, on American foreign policy, on Iraq, on Afghanistan. There was a substantive discussion about what it is about the nature of the American presence in the world that created a situation in which movements like al-Qaeda can thrive and prosper. I thought that was a very promising sign.
>
> But that discussion got short-circuited. Sometime in late October, early November 2001, the tone of the discussion switched and it became: What's wrong with the Islamic world that it failed to produce democracy, science, education, its own enlightenment, and created societies that breed terror?[26]

The attacks greatly strengthened the sense that the Enlightenment had to be defended. The political philosopher Stephen Bronner declared that:

> The 11th of September only highlights what should have been obvious: the need remains for an unrelenting assault on religious fanaticism not merely of the Islamic variety, but of the sort promulgated by 'born again' Christians, biblical literalists, Protestant sects intent on converting the Jewish infidels, and all those who would bring their revealed certainties – contested by others with other revealed certainties – into the mainstream of public life.[27]

From a very different ideological perspective,[28] David Kelley, the head of the Institute of Objectivist Studies, a right-wing libertarian group founded by the popular author Ayn Rand, also described the Enlightenment in terms of a very similar division between rational modernity and hate-filled enemies of 'reason, the pursuit of happiness, individualism, progress, and freedom'.[29] He believed that the attacks on New York should be understood primarily as an attack on enlightened modern culture and on America as the fullest embodiment of that culture:

> It was obvious to virtually everyone that the World Trade Center was targeted because it represented freedom, tolerance, innovation, commercial enterprise, the pursuit of happiness in this life. Our modernist values were thrown into sharp relief by the hatred they provoked in our enemies.[30]

Others on the Right were also happy to use the language of Enlightenment, arguing that the failure of the Arab Middle East to create suitably secular and peaceful societies meant that America had no choice but to bring stability and order to the region. In an article published in the *Weekly Standard* on 15 October, a little more than a month after the attacks, Max Boot, a prominent neoconservative historian, argued that 'Afghanistan and other troubled lands today cry out for the sort of enlightened foreign administration once provided by self-confident Englishmen in jodhpurs and pith helmets'.[31] After Afghanistan, he argued almost presciently, Iraq should be liberated and provided with the just administration it clearly could not create for itself.

Richard Lowry, the editor of the *National Review*, picked up on the need to bring Enlightenment to the people of Iraq in an article published on the same day as Boot's piece. After a US invasion and a UN Protectorate, Lowry called for the installation of 'an Iraqi government that one would hope would be thoroughly democratic – but that would at a minimum be pro-Western and capitalist'. This, he said, 'would represent a return to an enlightened paternalism toward the Third World, premised on the idea that the Arabs have failed miserably at self-government and need to start anew'.[32] Some of the thinkers associated with neoconservatism also called for a programme of democratization in the Middle East; it was in America's interests to promote democracy. Writing in *Foreign Affairs* in the early part of 2003, Thomas Carothers claimed that 'aggressive democracy promotion in the Arab world is a new article of faith among neoconservatives inside and outside the administration'.[33]

This theme – enlightened engagement to prevent future terrorist attacks – helped secure support for the invasion of Iraq from those on the Right who were disinclined to think in terms of a faith-based confrontation between Christianity and Islam, of revenge for 9/11 or of assassination attempts on Bush's father that may or may not have happened.[34]

Elements on the Right in America continue to construct the modern Enlightenment around the central struggle between reason and faith, especially in the context of the War on Terror. In the furore over the Danish cartoons of Muhammad in the early months of 2006, journalists reached back to the clichés of the eighteenth century to make sense of what looked like a clash of civilizations made flesh. Summing up much conservative opinion in the United States, David Brooks described the difference between the enlightened West and its Islamist opponents in a column in the *New York Times*:

> Our mindset is progressive and rational. Your mindset is pre-Enlightenment and mythological. In your worldview, history doesn't move forward through gradual understanding. In your worldview, history is resolved during the apocalyptic conflict between the supernaturally pure *jihadist* and the supernaturally evil Jew.[35]

The idea of Enlightenment helped reconcile allegedly responsible and serious liberal and left-wing intellectuals to the need to invade Iraq. In Britain, commentators pointed out how invasion would liberate the Iraqi people from a fascist tyrant, and they berated the anti-war movement for allowing its obsessive anti-Americanism to cause it to abandon its commitment to the Enlightenment. Writing in March 2002, the former editor of the *New Statesman* John Lloyd argued that 'the view . . . that in a consideration of action against Iraq the folly, imperialism and crimes of America are the only matters which may enter the discussion is an abdication of the left's own attachment to enlightenment rationalism'.[36]

Writing in the months before the March 2003 invasion of Iraq,

Independent columnist Johann Hari suggested that conservative opponents of the war were sceptical of American policy because they saw it as 'an overly optimistic Enlightenment project inimical to conservative values'.[37] Supporters of the war who identified with the progressive traditions of the Left could take comfort from their distance from the old-style conservative Right. After all, if Pat Buchanan and Henry Kissinger opposed invasion, how could one be progressive and not support it? In toppling tyrants in the Middle East, Hari argued, America was acting out of 'enlightened self-interest'.[38] Realism and its attempts to preserve the status quo would no longer serve, since client dictators 'had a vested interest in not educating their populations'.[39] A US invasion would serve the cause of human emancipation and act to bring Enlightenment to the region, since only democracy and education could effectively undermine the appeal of radical Islam and reduce the threat of terrorism in the future. American military power thus became an agent of enlightened progress.

Norman Geras, a Marxist academic and a central figure in Britain's pro-war Left, confirmed that the struggle for Enlightenment was at the heart of his understanding of contemporary politics. After 9/11 and the July 2005 bombings in London there could no longer be any doubt, as far as he was concerned, that the fundamental conflict in the twenty-first century was 'the battle for and against democratic societies, for and against pluralist, enlightenment cultures, being fought across the world today'.[40] When Geras and others sought to reach beyond the socialist Left to 'egalitarian liberals and others of unambiguous democratic commitment' through the publication of a 'broad statement of principles' called the Euston Manifesto, they laid claim to the legacy of the Enlightenment:

> We reject fear of modernity, fear of freedom, irrationalism, the subordination of women; we reaffirm the ideas that inspired the great rallying calls of the democratic revolutions of the eighteenth century: liberty, equality and solidarity; human rights, the pursuit of happiness.[41]

Concepts associated with the Enlightenment also feature in attempts by America's pro-war liberals to convince the Democrats to support the War on Terror. Writing in 2004, Peter Beinart complained that 'American liberalism, as defined by its activist organizations, remains largely what it was in the 1990s – a collection of domestic interests and concerns' even though 'totalitarian Islam has killed thousands of Americans and aims to kill millions'. If this totalitarian Islam gained power, Beinart claimed it would 'reign [sic] terror upon women, religious minorities, and anyone in the Muslim world with a thirst for modernity or freedom'.[42] The left-wing writer Paul Berman made a similar case for reviving liberal anti-totalitarianism in the context of the War on Terror.[43] 'Decent' or 'hard' liberals had fought a good Cold War; now it was time for a new generation to take up the challenge.

Christopher Hitchens felt comfortable talking about his 'temporary neocon allies'[44] on the grounds that they saw the need to deal with dictators like Milosevic, the Taliban and Saddam Hussein 'sooner rather than later'. Saddam Hussein and Osama bin Laden were, in Hitchens' view, the successors to the totalitarian dictators of the mid-twentieth century. They had to be resisted by a West confident of its values if further terrorist atrocities were to be prevented. Commenting on Fernando Botero's paintings based on the prisoner abuses in Abu Ghraib, Hitchens suggested that comparisons with Goya's painting *Second of May, 1808* were perhaps apt, since 'Goya was divided in his own mind between Spanish patriotism and a covert sympathy for the Napoleonic forces, which, even at second hand, were bringing the principles of 1789 to his own benighted state'.[45] The idea seems to be that the invasion of Iraq should provoke a similar ambivalence among thoughtful observers. On the one hand one can see how foreign occupation would upset Iraqi national feeling. But on the other hand, by invading Iraq the Americans are bringing the principles of 1776 to a benighted country, albeit at second hand. Spain, that lucky recipient of second-hand republican principles, was a fascist dictatorship as late as 1975. If Hitchens' analogy holds, the Iraqis can hope to achieve stable liberal democracy sometime after 2150.

Supporters of Anglo-American policies after 9/11 can draw on a model of Enlightenment that has become something like the conventional wisdom among intellectuals and commentators. This Enlightenment is understood above all in the context of a conflict between the rational and the irrational. Enlightenment is identified with reason in the broad sense of empirical inquiry and rational analysis. Its enemies are identified as 'those forces of religious reaction, conservative prejudice, and fascist irrationalism whose inspiration derived from . . . the Counter-Enlightenment'.[46] Enlightenment is associated closely with Western states that restrict the power of religious institutions and formally respect the freedom of the individual. The details of what is meant by Enlightenment are, however, often left rather vague. Some talismanic names and phrases crop up: Locke, Hume, Voltaire and Jefferson; the scientific method, the mind's adulthood, dare to know. But however it is described, Enlightenment is normally invoked in the context of a conflict with its external enemies: reason is threatened by faith, science is threatened by superstition, and so on.

This is what Stephen Bronner has called 'the great divide' of modern political life. In his emphasis on the clash of reason and unreason he echoes Karl Popper. Writing in *The Open Society and its Enemies*, Popper had claimed as long ago as 1945 that 'the conflict between rationalism and irrationalism has become the most important intellectual, and perhaps even moral, issue of our time'.[47] It is certainly true that Enlightenment is today most often talked about in the context of a confrontation with its irrational enemies. Enlightenment is something to be defended against, or brought to bear on, external irrational or anti-rational threats. The enemies of Enlightenment, the lyrics, vary, but the basic structure, the tune, remains the same. For this reason I will call models of Enlightenment that follow Bronner's organizing division of the rational and the irrational the Folk Enlightenment.

Stephen Bronner is a subtle and serious writer and his book *Reclaiming the Enlightenment* (2004) is in many respects exemplary,[48] but because his Enlightenment is built around opposition to openly irrational enemies, he ends up failing to recognize much more serious divisions in modern politics. For example, he speaks approvingly of the 'new anti-war and anti-globalization movements':

> The Enlightenment has always been – historically and politically – a force for securing liberty and fostering resistance against material oppression . . . These same ideals influenced the New Deal and the Popular Front. They became manifest in the attempt to transform the civil rights movement into a 'poor people's' movement and, even now, in the cosmopolitan sensibility of new anti-war and anti-globalization movements with their concern for international law and human rights.[49]

And yet he is also distressed at the lack of loyalty that global institutions enjoy from citizens and subjects:

> New 'bourgeois' international and transnational organizations are generating a huge bureaucracy and ever new powers for enforcing programs and laws, without simultaneously gaining the loyalty of subjects and citizens. That such institutions are the only available options for mitigating planetary problems of immigration, pollution, regional illnesses like AIDS and global poverty makes the lack of loyalty they exact from ordinary citizens all the more distressing.[50]

The global justice movement has sought precisely to destroy the legitimacy of at least some of the transnational organizations. It has done so through a distinctive combination of spectacular protest and reasoned argument. It argues that its opponents have betrayed the principles of the Enlightenment for the sake of corporate and state power. At the same time, the transnational institutions themselves have criticized the protestors' methods and have sought to depict them as simplistic, naive or vicious. They have been keen to denounce the protestors as fear-filled enemies of progress and unenlightened xenophobes. Each side claims to be presenting arguments based on fact, and both seek to persuade through appeals to universal principles of justice. The World Bank / IMF inside the convention centres and the clowns and the anarchists outside are calling for the creation of a humane social order, for a global system that fulfils the promise of Enlightenment. Both sides might be wrong, but they are definitely not both right, and a revived Enlightenment must decide between them or reject them both. A structure of Enlightenment that admits both because they both claim to be enlightened cannot be of central importance to our current politics. Their struggle marks a, perhaps the, 'great divide' in contemporary politics. Understood narrowly in terms of a clash between the rational and the irrational, the Enlightenment can say little about one of the most important political contests of our time.

This Folk Enlightenment precedes, and extends far beyond, the rhetoric of the War on Terror. In controversies concerning religion, culture and human rights, phrases from the eighteenth-century Enlightenment constantly crop up. Intellectuals, academics and policy-makers like to meet to discuss the meaning and relevance of Enlightenment.[51] Calls to defend the Enlightenment from a resurgent unreason recur in allegedly serious journalism. The historical Enlightenment also provides explicit or implicit justification for a substantial subgenre in modern publishing, the scientific polemic against religion.[52] Those in the English-speaking cultural and creative industries overwhelmingly identify themselves with 'Enlightenment values', as do scientific and technical elites. Scientists worry that their irrational enemies are growing in power and confidence. Media workers worry about the threat posed by fascists and other extremists.

The formal similarity between various expressions of the Folk Enlightenment obscures important differences between them. Left-wingers like Stephen Bronner talk about 'liberal and socialist forces imbued with the Enlightenment heritage', while those on the Right locate the spirit of Enlightenment among scientists and in the business community.[53] And the choice of irrational enemies also varies. Stephen Bronner extends and renovates Enlightenment antagonism to religion with a far-reaching critique of postmodernism and a stirring defence of science. But many would-be enlightened intellectuals stick with Evangelical Christianity and Islam as their preferred enemies, or more accurately, as the phenomena against which they can define Enlightenment. Writing in 2005, for example, Salman Rushdie boldly asserted that 'the Enlightenment wasn't a battle against the state but against the church'. The growing importance of religion in American politics, and the controversies over freedom of speech in matters of religious faith in Britain, suggest to Rushdie that the Enlightenment in the West is under threat. So much so that 'it seems we need to fight the battle for the Enlightenment again in Europe as well as in the United States'.[54]

Journalists can also earn a decent living with warnings about the threat posed to the Enlightenment inheritance by New Age spirituality, the modern craze for Eastern mysticism and the wilder shores of alternative medicine. Francis Wheen declared that the aim of his book *How Mumbo Jumbo Conquered the World* (2004) was 'to show how the humane values of the Enlightenment have been abandoned or betrayed, and why it matters; those who rewrite or romanticise history, like those who rejoice in this demise or irrelevance, are condemned to repeat it'.[55] He attacks those who advocate a 'revolt against reason'[56] and denounces 'those who refuse to learn from experience . . . whether they be holy warriors, anti-scientific relativists, economic fundamentalists, radical post-modernists, New Age mystics, or latter-day Chicken Lickens'.[57]

Although their beliefs are in some respects strikingly different from both Wheen's and each other's, the British writers Melanie Phillips and Polly Toynbee also characterize the Enlightenment in similar ways. Toynbee contrasts the values of Enlightenment with the 'demented killers lining up to murder in the name of God'[58] while Phillips talks of how 'our super-scientific age has seen a popular flight from science to New Age therapies such as faith-healing, energy-giving crystals or *feng shui*'.[59] The most pressing threat to Enlightenment differs according to taste and local political calculations – the mainstream Left likes to fret about religious fundamentalism, the Right tends to go after postmodernism – but the basic structure is the same. Enlightenment is reason and a commitment to science; its enemies are irrational. Both sides state clearly which side they are on and there is little room for confusion or ambiguity.

In *The March of Unreason* (2005), the British politician and intellectual Dick Taverne contrasts the enlightened scientific world-view with both religious fundamentalism and 'eco-fundamentalism'.[60] He describes the theme of his book as 'the conflict between the evidence-based approach and dogma' and argues for the pressing relevance of the Enlightenment struggle against unreason in the present day:

> The building blocks of today's liberal democracies were laid in the seventeenth and eighteenth centuries . . . It is no coincidence that this was the time when modern science was born. Indeed science was the chief progenitor of the Enlightenment. Both science and democracy are based on the rejection of dogmatism and whenever and wherever ideology rules, freedom as well as the evidence based approach is suppressed.[61]

Taverne's enemies of Enlightenment will be familiar by now, although he does throw in one or two more exotic ones. Along with fundamentalists, postmodernists and 'eco-fundamentalists', he is deeply troubled by the antics of organic farmers and homeopaths.

Not only is there broad agreement about how we should understand Enlightenment in the context of resistance to an irrational 'Counter-Enlightenment', there is also a widespread sense that these enemies are gaining in power and confidence.[62] David Kelley claims to believe that the effective defence of the Enlightenment is 'vital to the future of our civilization' and again there is extensive support for this idea on both sides of the Atlantic and among writers who would consider themselves bitterly opposed in political terms. Writing of the vanguard of this renewed assault on reason, Francis Wheen echoes the words of David Kelley, the heir of Ayn Rand, by declaring:

> Its leaders may seem an incongruous coalition – post-modernists and primitivists, New Age and Old Testament – but they have been remarkably effective over the past quarter-century. Nor are

they merely dunder-heads or fanatics who argue that 'ignorance is bliss' to assuage any prickings of guilt at their own imbecility; those who may know no better have been aided and abetted by a latter-day *trahison des clercs*.[63]

Taverne claims that 'religious fundamentalism is rampant, not only in Islam and among Jewish settlers in Palestine; in America we see the spread of creationism and the return to the beliefs that prevailed before the Enlightenment banished superstition and modern science was born.' Fundamentalism, he says, 'is a serious danger to peace and democracy. It spreads intolerance wherever it is found.'[64]

Frank Furedi, the British intellectual, goes further, warning of impending disaster:

> The cultural valuation of superstition over reason and the revival of ancient forms of mysticism testify to a profound crisis of meaning in contemporary society. We are no longer talking about isolated and marginal practices. The 'alternative' has gone mainstream and exercises formidable influence over our lives. Superstitious prejudice about the unique psychic power of holistic healers is systematically transmitted through popular culture. Ideas that were formerly associated with the esoteric – holistic, organic, psychic healing, cleansing, detoxing, rebirthing – now trip off our tongues.[65]

Writing about the widespread popular belief in conspiracy theories, Melanie Phillips warns that 'we are living through a flight from reason itself, a kind of collective paranoia. Unchecked, this can lead to dictatorship or totalitarianism as people no longer have the wherewithal to defend themselves against the lies that bring dictatorships to power.'[66] For Phillips and Taverne, and for many others, the defence of reason and the scientific method from its irrational enemies is central to the politics of our times. To be enlightened is to recognize this and order one's priorities accordingly. Otherwise democracy will decay along with the rest of the Enlightenment legacy.

Perhaps, argues David Kelley, we should create a 'Party of Modernity' – a group that self-consciously defends the Enlightenment from its pre- and postmodern enemies:

> We had a fleeting glimpse of such a party in the immediate aftermath of 9/11, when the terrorist threat to the values of modernity was denounced by commentators across the political spectrum, from Aryeh Neier to Charles Krauthammer, from the *New Republic* to the *Weekly Standard*. An enduring version of that consensus is possible. And it is vital for the future of our civilization.[67]

The idea that Enlightenment in the modern age should best be understood as the struggle between reason and faith gives form to the work of many other influential writers, as does the idea that the Enlightenment legacy faces a serious, possibly fatal, challenge from the resurgent forces of unreason. In Britain Kelley's Party of Modernity could count on John Lloyd, David Aaronovitch, Johann Hari and a number of other progressive writers, insofar as they see in the rise of political Islam, and left-wing apologies for it, a serious challenge to the Enlightenment heritage. In the United States Paul Berman and Peter Beinart take a similar line. Critics have attacked the Bush White House for its ideological and faith-based approach to politics, and Al Gore has complained about the Republican 'assault on reason'.[68] Yet the Republican administration has also invoked the language of Enlightenment to justify its War on Terror. In August 2003 President Bush denounced the bomb attack on UN headquarters in Baghdad, saying that those responsible had demonstrated 'their contempt for the innocent; their fear of progress and their hatred of peace'.[69] A month later the White House's *Progress Report on the Global War on Terrorism* used identical rhetoric:

> Murderous attacks in Bali, Jakarta, Mombasa, Riyadh, Casablanca, Jerusalem, Baghdad, and Najaf underscore terrorists' continued contempt for the innocent, their fear of progress, and their hatred of peace. The civilized world must remain vigilant and

committed to a long and critical struggle – until Americans and people around the world can lead their lives free from fear of terrorism.[70]

In November 2003 Colin Powell insisted that America would defeat the foreign terrorists 'who are coming to Iraq to visit their hatred and fear of progress on the Iraqi people and those who are trying to help them. We will find them wherever they are. And they will be destroyed'.[71] It appears that membership of Kelley's Party of Modernity is all but obligatory among the political classes.

In the field of science Richard Dawkins would also qualify. His determination to pit material science against religion neatly fits with the structure of the Folk Enlightenment. He agitates against religion because he says that 'it teaches us to be satisfied with not understanding the world', a patently untrue claim, but one that leaves him squarely in the Party of Modernity. Recently Dawkins announced that 'the enlightenment is under threat, so is reason, so is truth'. Accordingly he has set up the Richard Dawkins Society for Reason and Science to defend science from 'organized ignorance' and 'to go on the attack for the sake of reason and sanity'.[72] As with most defenders of the Enlightenment, Dawkins makes a clear and clean division between reason and the enemies that threaten it. Another scientist, Sam Harris, suggests in *The End of Faith* that 'it is time that scientists and other public intellectuals observed that the contest between faith and reason is zero-sum'. He believes that fundamentalism in itself poses a serious threat to world peace.[73] These two men are only the most prominent advocates of the Folk Enlightenment among scientists.

For much of the time, this Folk Enlightenment is the only one available.[74] It saturates our intellectual culture and informs many of our assumptions about public life. As a consequence political disputes about the distribution of resources are recast as metaphysical clashes between abstract nouns. Some of those who defend Enlightenment from its irrational enemies offer up 'the great divide' between faith and reason, rather than the old conflict between Left and Right, as the central organizing opposition of our time. Others maintain the Left/Right distinction by identifying their political opponents with the enemies of the Enlightenment. Enlightenment values can be described in ways that sound both left-wing and right-wing, and the threats to reason vary accordingly. But the central division, between the enlightened inheritance and the forces of unreason, constantly recurs. The lyrics vary, but the tune remains the same. So the Folk Enlightenment provides a structure both for Democrat attacks on Republicans and for Republican rhetoric about their War on Terror.

With a hint of proprietorial resentment, Francis Wheen has remarked on the way that this model pervades the intellectual culture:

> I've noticed the phrase or word 'mumbo jumbo' occurring a lot more these days . . . I don't know if that is anything to do with it being in the title of the book. Quite often I read newspapers and come across what I think might be echoes of the book, little references that make me think the writer has read it, particularly when I see it in conjunction with the words like 'retreat from reason' or 'enlightenment legacy'. Maybe a lot of people had this idea at the same time.[75]

As we have seen, the idea of a central conflict between self-declared defenders of the Enlightenment and self-declared enemies can be found in works that long pre-date Wheen's, but his book did go some way to extend its popular reach, especially in Britain. But are defenders of the Enlightenment correct? Does the Enlightenment tradition today face its most serious threat in 'the forces of unreason'? For the most part its self-styled defenders content themselves with listing their enemies and quoting some of the self-evidently inane things that some of them say. Although they claim that enlightened civilization is mortally threatened by the forces of unreason, they don't provide much evidence for this idea. Despite their ready access to the mainstream media, and the widespread support they enjoy among both elite groups and the general public, the defenders of Enlightenment feel threatened, even persecuted, by a resurgent unreason. Mockery of those who peddle sensational scare stories (those 'latter-day Chicken Lickens') is part of their enlightened *schtick*, but it never occurs to them that they might be in the same line of work. If we accept their claims, we are rewarded with a clear and simple division between the Enlightenment and its enemies: the free world is threatened by radical Islam and 'Arab rage'; secular society is threatened by Christian fundamentalism; science is threatened by postmodern relativism. Here, then, the lines are drawn and here we can take our stand. All this might be rhetorically effective and emotionally satisfying, but is it true?

It is time to look more closely at the historical Enlightenment, whose legacy is so vigorously, if vaguely, defended.

2

What Was Enlightenment?

Within limits, the Enlightenment was what one thinks it was.
Norman Hampson, *The Enlightenment* (1968)

VERSIONS OF ENLIGHTENMENT

Scholars disagree about exactly what the Enlightenment was, when it started and finished, where it began, and even if it happened at all. The philosopher Jonathan Rée contends that Enlightenment is best understood as an invention of nineteenth-century polemic, rather than as a self-conscious and coherent movement. He argues that Romantic writers conjured up an 'Enlightenment' located in the decades before the French Revolution that sought progress through the unpitying application of reason. They could then blame this Enlightenment for the Terror in France and contrast it with their own insistence on the central importance of sentiment.[1] Other scholars date the origins of the Enlightenment back to the period directly after the Glorious Revolution of 1688 in Britain. In this English-speaking Enlightenment the philosopher John Locke, the theorist of the limited and tolerant state, plays a central part.[2] Jonathan Israel also situates the Enlightenment in the last decades of the seventeenth century and the first decades of the eighteenth. But rather than concentrate on British scientists and philosophers, he identifies Enlightenment most especially with the career of the Jewish philosopher Baruch Spinoza and his assault on orthodox religion.[3] Yet another tradition continues to identify Enlightenment with the Age of Reason in France beginning in the 1740s, and sees Voltaire as the representative figure.[4]

The most influential recent case for making the British experience central to our understanding of Enlightenment is made by Roy Porter in his book, *Enlightenment: Britain and the Creation of the Modern World* (2001). Porter emphasizes the contribution of the great philosopher of religious toleration, John Locke, to later developments in Britain, France and the rest of the world. The mainstream of this British Enlightenment did not seek to overthrow an absolutist tyranny; rather it sought to justify and defend the limited monarchy introduced in 1688 and reinforced by the accession of George I in 1714. Locke and the other great figures of the period wrote and spoke in support of what Porter called 'a quadruple alliance of freedom, Protestantism, patriotism and prosperity'.[5]

Porter argues that in Britain Enlightenment was a reaction against the kinds of state activism that had driven the country to a succession of political emergencies. The ambitions of Charles I and James II for an absolute, Catholic monarchy, and the radical 'levelling' democracy of the New Model Army, had terrified the landed classes from the mid-seventeenth century onwards. The Protectorate under Oliver Cromwell had left them with little appetite for an unfettered executive. The limited Protestant monarchy of William III was a response to the twin dangers of monarchical tyranny and popular insurrection.

Locke established the theoretical justifications for the new social and political order. Central to it was a new conception of the state. Within certain limits, this state would no longer concern itself with the religious convictions of its citizens. It would demand only their bodily obedience to the law. The state could legitimately use force to defend the 'civil interests' of its citizens – 'life, liberty, health, and indolency of body; and the possession of outward things, such as money, lands, houses, furniture and the like'.[6] But it would no longer seek to rule over men's consciences or to interfere with the lawful enjoyment of property. Absolutism had sought to outlaw error by establishing a monopoly on truth in alliance with Catholic or Puritan religious authority. This move away from absolute, divinely sanctioned central authority coincided with a rejection of system in philosophy and a determination to remove, in Locke's words, 'some of the rubbish that lies in the way of knowledge'. Only the evidence of the senses could lead to knowledge, and only a community of free men could evaluate this knowledge. In place of the monarchy of system came the oligarchy of peer review.

A generation after Locke, David Hume attempted to extend the empirical method to the study of mind itself and sought to demonstrate the dominion of impressions over ideas, and of desire over reason. Like Locke, Hume championed the evidence of the senses and insisted that it provided the only basis for an adequate understanding of the world and of human nature. Far from promoting the tyrannical rationalism denounced by later critics, Hume dismissed the idea that reason alone could establish any kind of programme of action, much less provide a basis for morality: 'We speak not strictly and philosophically when we talk of the combat of passion and of reason. Reason is, and ought only to be, the slave of the passions and can never pretend to any other office than to serve and obey them . . .' In his insistence that reason is and ought to be the slave of the passions, Hume points the way to an effective critique of modern science. Rather than engaging in a paradoxical campaign against the 'tyranny of reason', we can inquire instead into the passions that employ scientific reason – passions that are themselves neither reasonable nor scientific.[7] As a central figure in the actual, historical Enlightenment in Britain, Hume makes it impossible for us to dismiss the various projects of the eighteenth century as a kind of rationalist frenzy. Those, like the British writer John Gray, who want to implicate the Enlightenment in the excesses of communism and fascism, can do so only by ignoring Hume and his many followers, who were acutely aware that we are passionate creatures, and that reason alone cannot provide an adequate basis for action.[8]

Hume has been enlisted by the modern Right as the emblem of a safely commonsensical British Enlightenment, and now serves in some circles as an idealized model of modern humanity: sociable and independent-minded, curious and sceptical, pleasure-seeking and prudent. But in eighteenth-century Britain, Hume's empiricism and his scepticism about religion made him an unusual, even freakish, figure; both Glasgow and Edinburgh universities distinguished themselves by turning down opportunities to employ the greatest philosopher in Scottish history. Boswell, Samuel Johnson's biographer, came to gawp at the great sceptic on his deathbed, goggling as Hume prepared for extinction without the consolation of the Church. Hume's sheer strangeness should warn us against assuming that any modern Enlightenment worthy of the name will find easy acceptance among cultural and political elites.

There is much that is appealing in the British Enlightenment's moderate and defensive liberalism and in Porter's portrait of it as the model of Enlightenment. His British Enlightenment is a convivial affair:

> The British avant-garde was not a network of persecuted rebels or underground samizdat authors, destined to hand down the torch of liberal democracy to Kennedy's America or Blair's Britain. They are better likened to the mixed clientele talking, talking, talking in a hot, smoky and crowded coffee house; men sharing broad convictions and sympathies, but differing, and agreeing to differ, on matters close to their hearts.

But when Porter suggests that 'the enlightened always wanted, nay, *expected* to have their pudding and eat it',[9] he downplays the menace that Hume and others posed to established opinions, and provides an eighteenth-century Britain that can be readily appropriated by self-declared inheritors of the Enlightenment. Pragmatic and stoutly empirical, these modern-day Humes avoid French-sounding abstractions. They enjoy their food and drink and the pleasures of society. They trust in the evidence of their senses and take care to avoid the wrong kinds of sensory impressions. The excitements of life in the Washington or Westminster media villages are made more piquant by the sense that these successful journalists and television historians have stepped into the shoes of giants. After all, if

Hume saw fit to reinvent himself as a practical man of letters and diplomat after the philosophical exertions of his youth, surely the young man who dispenses with philosophy entirely, and moves straight from a modern history degree at Oxford to the editorial pages of the *Daily Telegraph*, or from Harvard to a free-market think tank, is only showing an enlightened appetite for the good things available to us in this world.

Unlike the British Enlightenment, the French version had at its heart a liberationist project: the destruction of absolute and Catholic monarchy. From the mid-eighteenth century onwards the *philosophes*, the French champions of Enlightenment, agitated against the combination of religious and political despotism that Voltaire called *l'infâme*, the infamy. The *philosophes* drew heavily on British ideas in their struggle to reform France and they were generous in their praise of English society and politics. But whereas the innovations of Enlightenment figures in Britain strengthened the country's post-Civil War, especially after 1688, order, once exported they became imbued with revolutionary potential. Voltaire used the work of the English philosophers to promote himself and the ideals of liberation that he championed. He was, he claimed, 'the first man in France to explain Newton's discoveries'. And if Newton was correct, then the Enlightenment in France, which, according to its partisans, was nothing more than an elaboration of Newton's methods and discoveries, must be irresistible to all reasonable people. In Voltaire's work an idealized version of English society served as a form of rebuke to Catholic France; where the English honoured Newton, the French persecuted Descartes. His fellow philosophe Denis Diderot also developed the theme:

> In England, philosophers are honoured, respected; they rise to public offices, they are buried with the kings . . . In France warrants are issued against them; they are persecuted, pelted with pastoral letters . . . Do we see that England is any the worse for it?[10]

Peter Gay's book *The Enlightenment: An Interpretation* (1968) has done a good deal to establish the French *philosophes'* struggle against absolutism as the central event in the history of Enlightenment. In it he argues that 'in France the encounter with the establishment was most dramatic: in eighteenth-century France, abuses were glaring enough to invite the most scathing criticisms, while the machinery of repression was inefficient enough to permit critics adequate room for manoeuvre'. Such is his focus on France as the site of Enlightenment that he calls Voltaire 'the Newton of the Enlightenment'.[11] Porter and others might argue persuasively that Newton was the Newton of the Enlightenment. Indeed the great enemy of the Enlightenment, Friedrich Nietzsche, was in no doubt about where all the trouble started: 'What people call "modern ideas" or "the ideas of the eighteenth century" or French ideas – that in other words against which the German spirit has risen with a profound disgust – was of English origin.'[12]

Still, it is the confrontational and embattled Enlightenment in France that perhaps appeals most strongly to the proponents of the modern 'Folk Enlightenment'. Their dramatic conflict between reason and faith derives a certain amount of second-hand prestige from Voltaire's semi-clandestine struggle against judicial torture, the tyranny of Catholic cant and arbitrary power. Enlightenment in France sought the triumph of reason over the combined weight of hereditary monarchy and the Church. Its great divide, between reason in the service of liberation and superstition in the service of tyranny, nowadays acts as a model for secular critics of religion, for realist critics of postmodernism and for scientific critics of New Age therapies. In each instance, the heroic figure of Voltaire is to be found in the background. What many modern advocates of Enlightenment miss, however, is the sense in which Voltaire's campaign was against the tyrannical aspects of religion rather than against religious beliefs in and of themselves.[13] Voltaire himself was no atheist.

Writing in 1968, the British historian Norman Hampson pointed out that 'the attitudes which one chooses to regard as typical of the Enlightenment . . . constitute a free, subjective choice, which then, in turn, determines the shape of the synthesis one constructs for oneself'.[14] If we concentrate on the British Enlightenment, we tend to think in terms of a moderate and pragmatic attempt to defend society against political extremism. If we concentrate on French writers, the Enlightenment is better understood in terms of a campaign to put an end to political or religious tyranny. Whether the tone is defensive or aggressive, both are a conflict with external, irrational enemies. In their different styles both the British and the French Enlightenment inform and embolden the modern advocates of Folk Enlightenment.

BACON AND KANT

Taking Hampson at his word, we can describe another Enlightenment, one that speaks more directly to our present condition. We don't have to pretend that we have established exactly what the historical Enlightenment was, we only have to decide which attitudes from the seventeenth and eighteenth centuries might be helpful to us now. There are two thinkers, sometimes seen as being peripheral to the Enlightenment, who offer important insights into how we might become more fully enlightened – that is, how we might better understand the world and ourselves.

Both the British and French eighteenth-century thinkers took their cue from the scientific revolution of the seventeenth century and most especially from the work of Francis Bacon. A lawyer who spent most of his life in the service of Elizabeth I and James I, Bacon left public life in disgrace in 1621. But a generation after his death in 1626 his philosophical work was to become vastly influential. In Britain the Royal Society adopted Bacon as their emblem and regularly invoked him as their inspiration;[15] in France, the editors of the great *Encylopedie* called him 'the greatest, the most universal, and most eloquent of philosophers'.

In the preface to *The New Organum: or True Directions concerning the Interpretation of Nature* (1620), Bacon explained his ambitions. While it would be fine to discover some useful invention, it would be nobler to explain how such inventions might be found more surely in the future:

But above all, if a man could succeed, not in striking out some particular invention, however useful, but in kindling a light in nature – a light which should in its very rising touch and illuminate all the border-regions that confine upon the circle of our present knowledge; and so spreading further and further should presently disclose and bring into sight all that is most hidden and secret in the world, – that man (I thought) would be the benefactor indeed of the human race, – the propagator of man's empire over the universe, the champion of liberty, the conqueror and subduer of necessities.

Bacon's plan to advance knowledge and bring material improvement to mankind was at once practical and theoretical. At the level of theory, he sought to clarify the business of inquiry by removing all that was beside the point:

Men have been kept back, as by a kind of enchantment, from progress in the sciences by reverence for antiquity, by the authority of men accounted great in philosophy, and then by general consent.[16]

Man must inquire into the workings of nature without reference to what classical philosophy (in particular Aristotle) or the conventional wisdom said that he would find. Only in this way would the moderns surpass the ancients and come to mastery over nature. Rather than some scholastic or theological system of understanding, the new science envisaged by Bacon would depend on the experimental method. That is, the new scientist would inquire into nature and seek to discover by experiment the principles that governed the natural world; in this way, we would move steadily from a secure basis in observable fact to formulate general rules. Although it is not much commented on, this move away from system-building to an evidence-based approach drew heavily on the magical tradition. Bacon himself recognized the connection, and declared that 'the aim of magic is to recall natural philosophy from the vanity of speculations to the importance of experiments'.[17] The magical tradition had recorded a great number of resemblances in nature – the 'weeping' willow indicated that its bark would provide relief from pain, for example. These resemblances provided Bacon with a guide for experimentation that did not threaten to overwhelm empirical results with some abstract system of holistic explanation. The experimenter could isolate and explore suggestive resemblances from nature. Did the brain-like walnut help in the treatment of mental disorders, for example? True correspondences could be confirmed and false ones discarded once and for all. It is commonplace to describe magic as failed science. It might be more accurate to call science successful magic. This experimental method would have to overcome the long-standing prejudices of philosophers that 'the dignity of the human mind is impaired by long and close intercourse with experiments and particulars, subject to sense and bound in matter; especially as they are laborious to search, ignoble to meditate, harsh to deliver, illiberal to practise, infinite in number, and minute in subtlety'.[18] The advancement of learning would not come from the godlike exercise of theoretical reasoning, but from the patient taking of experimental pains.

Histories of the Enlightenment tend to mention Bacon only in passing or to refer vaguely to 'Baconianism' before hurrying on to the history of the Glorious Revolution or the salons of pre-revolutionary France.[19] And he is a problematic figure. His desire to discover and share knowledge for the general good runs alongside a willingness to employ torture in the service of his king.[20] It is awkward, too, that the father of experimental science drew on the techniques and lore of magic. Bacon insisted that experience should inform our understanding at a time when religious and scholastic preconceptions still saturated the experience of the world; it was his paradoxical triumph to employ magic for the purposes of disenchantment. But in Bacon we find the zeal for progress that characterizes the Enlightenment and the explicit connection between increased control over nature and increased liberty for mankind. The pursuit of the truth was both a practical and moral project. Even more than the British desire for stability or the French desire for change, this is the stuff of Enlightenment.

Without any overriding 'opinions and dogmas' to guide the natural philosopher, Bacon imagined that inquiry would be a matter of trial and error on the grand scale, and he saw the need for an institutional alliance between the state and the natural philosophers. The Royal Society and the later Anglo-American *condominia* between the state and scientific institutions are the culmination of his desire to see the establishment of man's empire over nature. Bacon is the prophet of the military-industrial complex, a fact that becomes more troubling when we bear in mind that he was also a finder and keeper of secrets and an enthusiastic servant of power. Indeed Bacon, with his desire to reconcile service to mankind with service to his monarch, is pregnant with the central conflict of Enlightenment between those who champion an Enlightenment of open and free inquiry, a campaign that is bound up with a programme of liberation from tyranny, and those who pursue Enlightenment in secret, in the service of unaccountable power. His influence can be found not only in the universities, but in the research facilities of the Pentagon and the Ministry of Defence. Let us call these conflicting impulses the 'Open Enlightenment' and, in homage to Bacon's magical preoccupations, the 'Occult Enlightenment'.

The seventeenth-century biographer and diarist John Evelyn claims that Bacon's magical intuitions were the death of him. Struck by the resemblance between salt and snow, he sought to find out if refrigeration would keep meat fresh:

> As he was taking the air in a coach with Dr Witherborne (a Scotchman, physician to the King) towards Highgate, snow lay on the ground, and it came into my Lord's thoughts, why flesh might not be preserved in snow, as in salt. They resolved to try the experiment at once. They alighted out of the coach and went into a poor woman's house at the bottom of Highgate Hill, and bought a hen, and made the woman gut it, and then stuffed the body with snow, and my Lord did help to do it himself. The

snow so chilled him that he immediately fell so extremely ill, that he could not return to his lodgings (I suppose at Gray's Inn), but went to the Earl of Arundel's house at Highgate.[21]

Appropriately enough, given the scientific controversies that now surround the industrial food economy, Bacon died while trying to freeze a chicken.

Bacon insists that we will only learn the truth about the world if we put away our preconceptions, whether they derive from our own preferences, or from established sources of authority. In the inquiry into nature Bacon's successors have been amazingly successful. Now in the urgent work of understanding the social world we should, like Bacon, reject established authority and our own inclinations, and be willing to pursue lines of inquiry associated with disreputable schools of thought. We ignore or downplay too many facts about the world on the grounds that they conflict with our settled convictions. Bacon insists that we construct our understanding of the world on facts alone, no matter how inconvenient they might be, even if this means breaking with systems of belief that provide us with stability and respectability. Bacon himself was prepared to seek Enlightenment in the magical tradition and risk allegations of witchcraft and devil worship. If we believe that authority illegitimately seeks to control our understanding of the world then Bacon speaks to us now as urgently as he spoke to the natural philosophers of the late seventeenth century. He tells us surely to follow the facts where they lead, without regard for established explanations, however venerable. For, like nature, society 'to be commanded must be obeyed'; we cannot presume to understand without study.

For all his powers of prophecy, Bacon could not see the conflict that would emerge between truth and other forms of power. In his time the state took little interest in the promotion of scientific inquiry, and the tension between what science might discover and the interests of the powerful had yet to be felt. But writing more than 150 years after Bacon's death at the eastern edge of Protestant Europe in the highly militarized kingdom of Prussia, Immanuel

Kant understood that the simple elision of the interests of the state and of mankind could not stand. English writers often affect to find Kant marginal – in his *Enlightenment*, Roy Porter dismisses Kant's ideal of freedom, calling it 'as timid as the man himself'[22] – but Kant's essay 'What is Enlightenment?' is the boldest and clearest description of what complete Enlightenment might in fact mean. Kant is far removed from the garrulous coffee-drinkers of Georgian London, but Porter was quite wrong to imagine that our understanding of Enlightenment can be adequate without him.

Writing as a subject of the avowedly enlightened King of Prussia, Frederick the Great, a few years before the revolution in France, Kant was able to draw on more than a century of philosophical writing from a number of national traditions. He does not seek to describe Enlightenment as one side of a confrontation between reason and unreason. Instead, he defines it as an individual's decision for personal autonomy, the decision to become intellectually adult:

> Enlightenment is man's release from his self-incurred tutelage. Tutelage is man's inability to make use of his understanding without direction from another. Self-incurred is this tutelage when its cause lies not in lack of reason but in lack of resolution and courage to use it without direction from another. *Sapere aude!* 'Have courage to use your own reason' – that is the motto of enlightenment.[23]

This much is quite familiar. *Sapere aude* has become a cliché of Enlightenment. But the short essay becomes more compelling and more exotic as it progresses. Kant not only explains what Enlightenment is, he explains how it might be achieved. He was sure that the adult use of reason is easier to achieve than our masters would have us believe:

> After the guardians have first made their domestic cattle dumb and have made sure that these placid creatures will not dare take a single step without the harness of the cart to which they are confined, the guardians then show them the danger which

threatens if they try to go alone. Actually, however, this danger is not so great, for by falling a few times they would finally learn to walk alone. But an example of this failure makes them timid and ordinarily frightens them away from further trials.[24]

For Kant, then, it is not the deep difficulty of living as an independently reasonable agent that prevents us from doing so; it is the carefully encouraged fear of what will happen if we stop accepting the strictures and the stories of the 'guardians' as the basis for our beliefs about the world. They show us what happens to those who fail, and discourage us from attempting the task ourselves.[25]

Kant optimistically claimed that general Enlightenment was consistent with political monarchy; the interests of the enlightened king would necessarily coincide with those of his enlightened subjects.[26] Besides, as far as Kant was concerned, the mere change of the political order would not bring about enlightenment. Unless the people have achieved a high level of independent understanding, any new set of governors will find another language with which to bamboozle and cajole us into obedience:

Perhaps a fall of personal despotism or of avaricious or tyrannical oppression may be accomplished by revolution, but never a true reform in ways of thinking. Rather, new prejudices will serve as well as old ones to harness the great unthinking masses.[27]

He argues that it is possible to avoid lawlessness in an enlightened society if a simple, though apparently counter-intuitive, distinction is made between the 'private' and the 'public' use of reason:[28]

The public use of one's reason must always be free, and it alone can bring about enlightenment among men. The private use of one's reason, on the other hand, may often be very narrowly restricted without particularly hindering the progress of enlightenment. By public use of one's reason I understand the use which a person makes of it as a scholar before the reading public. Private

use I call that which one may make of it in a particular civil post
or office which is intrusted to him.[29]

As an example, Kant describes a clergyman who must, as a duty to
his Church, conform with its doctrines in the conduct of his work.
In his 'public' capacity he may pursue the truth and speak freely
about it. As long as he believes that the principles of the sect he
represents *might* be true and that nothing in them is 'contradictory to
religion', he can perform his work conscientiously. But, Kant notes,
if the rules of his church are 'contradictory to religion' he must give
up his post. Kant chooses to focus on religion for a reason:

> I have placed the main point of Enlightenment – the escape of
> men from their self-incurred tutelage – chiefly in matters of
> religion because our rulers have no interest in playing the
> guardian with respect to the arts and sciences and also because
> religious incompetence is not only the most harmful but also the
> most degrading of all.[30]

As far as Kant is concerned, public reason must take precedence
over our private interests. If we cannot reconcile what we are
required to say in our 'private' capacity as workers with the
discoveries we make as free-thinking researchers exercising 'public'
reason, we must renounce the work we do, and with it the position
we hold in society. For Kant, Enlightenment entails a particular
attitude towards the truth. It requires that we defend and promote
truth, even if it conflicts with our own interests. Under conditions
of Enlightenment, truth becomes a moral concern.

Implicit in Kant's insistence on the primacy of personal conscience over institutional duty in religious matters is an Enlightenment that extends into every aspect of public life. Like some
modern atheists, Kant considers religion central to the question of
Enlightenment. To accept the opinions of others in religious
matters was, for Kant, evidence of a degrading immaturity of mind.
And in the eighteenth century it was in matters of religion that the
guardians of the state worked hardest to maintain our state of

tutelage. But modern state power in Britain and America does not concern itself much with enforcing uniformity of religious belief. For the most part we do not obey our leaders because we believe they have been chosen by God to rule over us. We accept the legitimacy of our modern guardians because of what we believe about material reality.

Our guardians expend a great deal of effort insulating their descriptions of the world from reasoned inquiry, since it is through their control of the public's understanding in this respect that they secure our obedience and maintain their position. Science, not theology, has become the arena in which we must fight for the victory of Enlightenment since it is through their claims to rationality and scientific understanding that our guardians bind us in obedience to the established order.

Between them, Kant and Bacon provide us both with a working model of what Enlightenment might mean – knowledge in the service of liberation – and with a method by which this might be achieved – the abolition of all that is beside the point and the creation of an impartial, 'public' programme of inquiry. There is little room in this version of Enlightenment for the clearly defined 'great divide' between reason and its enemies. This will seem strange to some readers. So in the following chapters I turn to the alleged 'threats to reason' presented by the defenders of today's Folk Enlightenment. My aim is to show that mental adulthood is not possible if we exaggerate the importance, or misunderstand the nature, of the forces of unreason. When we have finished, I hope that the way will be left clear for a revised understanding of what it would mean to be enlightened. It is high time we took a hammer to the Folk Enlightenment.

3

The Menace in the East

I don't know where bin Laden is. I have no idea and really don't care.
It's not that important. It's not our priority.
George W. Bush, 13 March 2003

We have already seen how the response to 9/11 drew on ideas associated with the Enlightenment. The United States represented modernity and freedom while its enemies were hate-filled adherents to a medieval world-view. This model, with its clean division between the rational and the irrational, expresses the assumptions of the Folk Enlightenment. It takes for granted the world-historical significance of conflict between secular modernity and fundamentalist reaction, and it insists that what motivates radical Islam is hostility to modernity. Those who planned the attacks on New York and Washington did not do so out of strategic calculation; rather, they acted out of psychosexual anxiety and hatred of freedom. Writing soon after the attacks, Christopher Hitchens, one of the most prominent secular liberal supporters of Western military intervention, emphasized that it was the good things about the West that infuriated the terrorists who attacked New York:

> Now is as good a time as ever to revisit the history of the Crusades, or the sorry history of partition in Kashmir, or the woes of the Chechens and Kosovars. But the bombers of Manhattan represent fascism with an Islamic face, and there's no point in any euphemism about it. What they abominate about 'the West,' to

put it in a phrase, is not what Western liberals don't like and can't defend about their own system, but what they *do* like about it and must defend: its emancipated women, its scientific inquiry, its separation of religion from the state. Loose talk about chickens coming home to roost is the moral equivalent of the hateful garbage emitted by Falwell and Robertson, and exhibits about the same intellectual content.[1]

Four years later, the same claim was being made by another secular liberal and self-styled progressive, Sasha Abramsky:

> We should attend to the way bin Laden and his followers invoke 'the West.' They do so alternately to describe any expansive and domineering First World economic and political system and, even more ominously, to demarcate a set of ostensibly decadent liberal political, cultural, social, and religious beliefs and practices. Indeed, what Al Qaeda apparently hates most about 'the West' are its best points: the pluralism, the rationalism, individual liberty, the emancipation of women, the openness and social dynamism that represent the strongest legacy of the Enlightenment. These values stand in counterpoint to the tyrannical social code idealized by Al Qaeda and by related political groupings such as Afghanistan's Taliban.[2]

This way of framing the War on Terror, in terms of a struggle between modernity and reaction, has informed recent attempts by intellectuals associated with the Democrat Party in the USA to construct a 'fighting faith', a progressive strategy for defeating terrorism. Paul Berman argues that:

> In the last couple of centuries, a new kind of society has emerged – a society that tries to encourage individual freedom, and tries to keep religion and government in separate corners, and to encourage open debate, and in those several ways to inculcate public habits of rational decision-making.[3]

This 'new kind of society', rooted in the ideals of the Enlightenment, defeated its totalitarian enemies in the twentieth century – the fascists, Phalangists, Nazis and finally the Soviet Communists. Now Berman urges us to face up to the new threat to the enlightened inheritance, Islamist terrorism.

Berman can only persuade us that we face a struggle analogous to the Second World War or the Cold War if the terrorists who attacked the United States on 11 September 2003 bear comparison with previous totalitarian movements, especially Nazism and Soviet Communism. Accordingly he claims that America and the West in general face a 'mass movement of radical Islamists'[4] who are 'drunk on the idea of slaughter'[5]. But while al Qaeda's leadership can plausibly be described as being 'drunk on the idea of slaughter', the tiny group of conspirators who launched the 9/11 attacks were never able to rely on mass public support. Instead they were funded by elements in Saudi Arabia's ruling elite. This country does plausibly imitate a totalitarian state of the old school, down to its rabid anti-Jewish propaganda, its blithe indifference to legal due process, its public executions and ferocious religious intolerance. But far from being America's main enemy in the War on Terror, 'Islamo-fascist' Saudi Arabia, along with neo-Stalinist Uzbekistan, is a staunch ally. America can hardly invade either country since they are both already host to substantial US garrisons. Peter Beinart, the former editor of the *New Republic*, argues in a similar vein to Berman, and tries to resuscitate liberal anti-totalitarianism in a new global struggle against terrorist extremism. Like Berman, Beinart manages to establish that Sayyid Qutb, one of the founding theorists of modern Islamism, was a strange and troubled man, but he does even less than Berman to establish al Qaeda as a plausible successor to America's Cold War enemy.[6]

In a long article published in September 2006, the British novelist Martin Amis also echoes Berman's argument. He sees in Islamist terrorism an irrational death cult, an amalgam of medieval ignorance and modern totalitarianism: 'Millennial Islamism is an ideology superimposed upon a religion – illusion upon illusion. It is not merely violent in tendency. Violence is all that is there.' It is pointless to consider the causes of the 9/11 attacks: 'we are not dealing in reasons because we are not dealing in reason'. Our only rational response to suicide-mass murder is 'something like an unvarying factory siren of unanimous disgust'.[7] Amis feels that this tactic goes beyond terrorism to something he calls 'horrorism'. He later tried to explain the distinction between 'horrorism' and 'terrorism':

> If for some reason you were about to cross Siberia by sleigh, you would be feeling 'anxiety'; when you heard the first howl of the wolves, your anxiety would be promoted to 'fear'; as the pack drew near and gave chase, your fear would become 'terror'; 'horror' is reserved for when the wolves are actually there. Some acts of terrorism are merely terrible. Suicide-mass murder, the act of self-bespattering, in which your assailant's blood and bones and organs become part of the argument, is always horrible.[8]

It is difficult to know what to make of this, except to note that horrible acts do not need to involve suicidal Islamists, or wolves. The agents of Western states have frequently committed horrible acts. 'Horrorism' took place in Dublin in 1974 and in Bologna in 1980; and these are only a couple of peacetime retail operations. We don't even bother to use words like 'terror' or 'horror' to describe the really large-scale productions. We prefer 'shock' and 'awe'.

And the 'unvarying factory siren of unanimous disgust' is not a 'rational response' to suicide-mass murder. It is an abandonment of rational inquiry, a flight to comforting fantasies about 'death cults'. To respond rationally to the suicide bomber is to ask how such a thing is made, how a human being can be programmed to destroy itself and others. What methods of indoctrination and emotional manipulation are used? How much does it cost? What resources are needed? Where did the techniques originate? Such questions might lead us briefly to the Old Man of the Mountains and his *hashisheen*. But if we are serious about daring to know, we will soon find ourselves in a world of experiments conducted without consent in lunatic asylums, and files destroyed on the orders of the Director of

Central Intelligence. We will find ourselves in a world of luminously disreputable acronyms and code words: MK–ULTRA and Bluebird.[9]

As an account of contemporary political reality this Folk Enlightenment version of the War on Terror has always run parallel with another family of explanations. Fundamentalist Christians in the United States can hardly condemn Koranic literalism on enlightened grounds. For them the War on Terror has always been a confrontation between two religions. In October 2002 Jerry Falwell declared that 'I think Mohammed was a terrorist . . . Jesus set the example for love, as did Moses. And I think that Mohammed set an opposite example'.[10] Ed McAteer, a co-founder of the Moral Majority and often called the 'Godfather of the Religious Right', believed that Arabs and Muslims were descended from Ishmael, the son of Abraham who was promised great wealth but would never be satisfied with what he had:

Find an Arab 6 feet, 4 inches tall, have him as handsome as Clark Gable. Give him a body like Charles Atlas. Give him the title to a $50 million mansion. Put him $100 million in the bank. And then, so that his resources will not be diminished, give him the title to 50 gushing oil wells. That man should be the ideal happy man, but he's a Muslim. Have him stand on a little piece of geography called Israel that backs up between the Dead Sea and the Mediterranean Sea, and if he sees a Jew walk by, with all he's got, all his happiness diminishes. He's got fever in his soul.[11]

In March 2006, in response to demonstrations in the Middle East, Pat Robertson said that 'these people are crazed fanatics, and I want to say it now: I believe it's motivated by demonic power. It is Satanic and it's time we recognize what we're dealing with . . . And the goal of Islam, ladies and gentlemen, whether you like it or not, is world domination. And, by the way, Islam is not a religion of peace.'[12]

This crusading mindset is popular in the military. In 2003 Lieutenant-General William G. Boykin, Deputy Undersecretary of Defense for Intelligence, stated that in the War on Terror 'the enemy is a guy named Satan'. Referring to his experiences fighting in Somalia, Boykin also said that 'I knew my God was bigger than his. I knew that my God was a real God and his was an idol'.[13] A battalion commander in the American assault on Fallujah, Lieutenant-Colonel Gareth Brandl, announced a year later in November 2004 that 'The marines that I have had wounded over the past five months have been attacked by a faceless enemy . . . But the enemy has got a face. He's called Satan. He lives in Fallujah. And we're going to destroy him.'[14]

The co-existence of both secular and religious justifications for the idea that we face a War on Terror closely resembles Western propaganda during the Cold War. The American state then promoted distinct themes in what the National Security Council called 'the fundamental conflict in the realm of ideas' between the idea of slavery and the idea of freedom.[15] Freedom could take a specifically religious tone, as when the Evangelical preacher Billy Graham wrote in 1954 that 'Either Communism must die, or Christianity must die, because it is actually a battle between Christ and the anti-Christ.'[16] Graham had come to prominence in 1949 during his 'Los Angeles crusade', a series of tent meetings. Both William Randolph Hearst, the newspaper magnate, and Henry Luce, the head of *Time* and *Fortune* magazines, decided to promote the previously obscure preacher. Hearst even sent a telegram to his editors instructing them to 'puff Graham'.[17] In his career he spoke to an estimated 210 million people in more than 180 countries.[18] His work helped enormously in sustaining America's international reputation as the defender of both personal and religious freedom.

In Latin America at the same time, the defence of liberty meant defending local ruling elites and American corporations from the demands of the public. In extreme cases, America justified its support for fascist dictatorships on the grounds that they were 'authoritarian' and not 'totalitarian'; they sought to control the behaviour of the population, but did not seek to control their minds. America could be justified in supporting authoritarian regimes if it served 'the defense of liberty and the national interest'.[19] Meanwhile in Europe during the Cold War, the American state was working with secular European intellectuals to popularize the struggle for cultural freedom and individualism against the conformist and culturally moribund Soviet Union; the West was all abstract expressionism and the heroic individual, the East was socialist realism and the bureaucratization of artistic production. During the Cold War, the defence of freedom could range from patronage of the arts and support for social democracy in Europe to the training of death squads in Latin America. It all depended on what best served American interests.

Berman and others have hesitated to revive the distinction between the totalitarian and the authoritarian, perhaps because Saudi Arabia under al-Qaeda would be no more or less 'totalitarian' than it is at present. In other words, no serious ideological distinction can be made between al-Qaeda and Saudi Arabia's current regime. They differ only in their attitude to American state power.

Freedom remains prominent in the rhetoric surrounding the War on Terror, whether the register is 'enlightened' or religious. In October 2001 the wife of the British Prime Minister, Cherie Blair, declared that 'we need to help Afghan women free their spirit and give them their voice back, so they can create the better Afghanistan we all want to see'. A month later, following the US invasion, George Bush was claiming that 'women now come out of their homes from house arrest'.[20] The official name for America's invasion of Iraq was Operation Iraqi Freedom.

Both religious and enlightened justifications for Western intervention in the Middle East since 2001 face an apparently unanswerable challenge from reality. We don't need to consider the fact of America's long-standing military domination of the region. We can leave to one side the fact that many of America's allies in the Middle East are 'Islamo-Fascists' and that the most important one, Saudi Arabia, takes its hostility to Christianity to truly extraordinary levels. We can also ignore America's long-term policy of supporting theocratic monarchy against secular nationalism in the interests of stability, which itself seems to be code for continued control of the region and its resources. The US administration is most concerned to establish the War on Terror as a long-term, even permanent, fact of life. This, more than any other war aim, is their overriding priority. Their interest in a crusade for Jesus or Enlightenment is strictly rhetorical. In 2001 the then Secretary of Defense, Donald Rumsfeld, provided an honest and accurate account of what would constitute victory in the War on Terror:

> Now what is victory? I say that victory is persuading the American people and the rest of the world that this is not a quick matter that's going to be over in a month or a year or even five years. It is something that we need to do so that we can continue to live in a world with powerful weapons and with people who are willing to use those powerful weapons. And we can do that as a country. And that would be a victory in my view.[21]

So the War on Terror will not end for the foreseeable future and victory means reconciling the American people to this new reality of permanent conflict. Accordingly, planners and conservative writers have started talking about a 'Long War', even a 'Millennium War', instead of a War on Terror.[22] In July 2006 the former House Speaker, Newt Gingrich, tried out the idea that we were now fighting 'World War III'. Referring not only to the situation in the Middle East but also to terrorist attacks in India, the threat of missile strikes from Cuba and the danger posed by North Korea, Gingrich told *Time* magazine that 'I think the clarity of the term "Third World War" is enormously helpful'.[23]

American actions since 2001 provide strong confirmation that the point of the War on Terror is to justify permanent warfare. Instead of addressing real problems of extremist violence and criminal activity in the world, the US state has invaded Afghanistan and Iraq and created humanitarian disasters in both those countries. It has increased its military presence in Central Asia and Central America and has announced that it intends to integrate more fully with friendly states – the Pentagon plans to 'become as adept at working with interior ministries as it is with defence ministries'.[24]

The US has identified Osama bin Laden as the mastermind behind the attacks, but by its own admission it is not trying very hard to capture him. As it stands, his own claims of responsibility are little more than prank phone calls. The Americans haven't brought any of the terrorist financiers to trial, nor have they investigated the extensive evidence of co-operation between the jihadis and Western intelligence and their allies in the years prior to 9/11. The CIA has the alleged operational planner of the attacks, Khalid Sheikh Mohammed, in custody. But they are trying to find ways to keep him out of open court.[25] More than five years after the attacks the man suspected of one of the most spectacular acts of terrorism in history remains at an undisclosed location, subject to an unknown regime of cognitive reorientation at the hands of the CIA and its contractors.

All in all, seen as a response to a threat to the security of the United States, the actions of the Bush White House since September 2001 are a series of murderous non sequiturs – but as an exercise in force projection in which the story of a War on Terror serves to justify their actions, they make perfect sense. American policy, and especially the invasion of Iraq, has undoubtedly made the world more dangerous. But while American state planners would doubtless prefer the world to be safe for American citizens, their first priority is to ensure that the American state and its main constituency, the American business class, retain a dominant position in the global system. A certain amount of tension is perhaps helpful in their efforts to convince the American people of the need for permanent warfare. We will see vigorous attempts to establish the unrepresentative nature of the Bush White House in the next few years. Republican and Democrat presidential candidates are hastening to distance themselves from Cheney and Rumsfeld, and from the Iraq war that many of them once supported. But it is not at all certain that American interventions in the Middle East will end with the arrival of a new administration. Indeed, responsible intellectuals are trying hard to find a nominally liberal basis on which to continue the War on Terror; it is in this light that we must read the likes of Peter Beinart and Paul Berman.

Enlightened supporters of the war, sincere enemies of fascism with an Islamic face, might want to insist that their support is only tactical, an alliance of convenience. They don't care what Rumsfeld and Cheney want; they want to see peace and justice spread throughout the Middle East. Perhaps they take the long view, the historically sophisticated and the morally responsible view. More than 500,000 people have died in Iraq, only one front in the War on Terror.[26] As I write the Americans have begun air-strikes in Somalia. They claim they are trying to kill men they *suspect* of involvement in terrorist attacks on US embassies in Africa.[27] They are targeting these suspects with C-130 transport planes that fire thousands of rounds per minute from high altitudes. What kind of campaign against terrorist extremism can possibly be advanced by the use of airborne cannons and howitzers on densely populated areas? Just how morally responsible and historically sophisticated do the advocates of the War on Terror expect us to be?

No element of the rhetoric surrounding the War on Terror can survive careful, actually enlightened inquiry. As a description of reality it amounts to a well-organized fraud, a piece of enchant-ment. It is as an attempt to reconcile the world to permanent war. In current circumstances, the language of Enlightenment itself, the language of universal human rights and modernity, has been successfully reduced to the stuff of world-historical kitsch, on a par with the apocalyptic fantasies of America's benighted and confused Evangelicals. In this way, Enlightenment provides cover, and perhaps comfort, for a ruling class that no longer feels able to function in conditions of peacetime democracy and requires instead the resources of an ongoing emergency.

4

Faith versus Reason

*A little philosophy inclineth a man's mind to atheism, but depth in
philosophy bringeth men's minds about to religion.*
                              Francis Bacon, 'Of atheism', *Essays* (1625)

Many of those who want to defend the Enlightenment from its
irrational enemies spend a great deal of time and energy worrying
about the power and influence of religion. Aside from the
mysterious suicide–murder cults of the Middle East they especially
worry about Evangelical and fundamentalist religion in the United
States. It is worth quoting in some detail from the founding
statement of the Richard Dawkins Foundation for Reason and
Science:

> A recent Gallup poll concluded that nearly 50% of the American
> public believes the universe is less than 10,000 years old . . . They
> believe this because they rate a particular bronze age origin myth
> more highly than all the scientific evidence in the world . . .
> Now, in the 21st century as we approach Darwin's bicentenary,
> the fact that half of Americans take Genesis literally is nothing less
> than an educational scandal.
>
> The enlightenment is under threat. So is reason. So is truth. So
> is science, especially in the schools of America. I am one of those
> scientists who feels that it is no longer enough just to get on and
> do science. We have to devote a significant proportion of our
> time and resources to defending it from deliberate attack from

organized ignorance. We even have to go out on the attack ourselves, for the sake of reason and sanity.[1]

In a lecture entitled 'Can the internet save the Enlightenment', the Nobel Prize-winning chemist Sir Henry Kroto declared that his world, the enlightened world of science and reason, was 'under attack'[2] from religion. The American scientist Sam Harris goes even further and declares that 'our technical advances in the art of war have finally rendered our religious differences – and hence our religious beliefs – antithetical to our survival'.[3] If we are to survive as a species we must put an 'end to faith' – it is as serious as that, according to Harris.

And it isn't just fundamentalism that troubles these critics of religion. Harris argues that 'religious moderates are, in large part, responsible for the religious conflict in our world, because their beliefs provide the context in which scriptural literalism and religious violence can never be adequately opposed'.[4] In his lecture, Kroto stated that there is 'no qualitative difference between the levels of irrationality' in philanthropic and kind-hearted expressions of religion and violent fundamentalism.

For the sake of clarity we ought to distinguish between two objections to religion. Firstly, its critics complain that it is irrational – 'delusional' is Dawkins' word. It must therefore be resisted by those who seek to defend the tradition of the Enlightenment: 'Faith is the great cop-out, the great excuse to evade the need to think and evaluate evidence. Faith is belief in spite of, even perhaps because of, the lack of evidence.'[5] Secondly, religion, and especially fundamentalist religion, has pernicious social effects: belief in the literal truth of the Bible sanctions murderous aggression and all manner of mayhem. As Sam Harris puts it, 'certainty about the next life is simply not compatible with tolerance in this one'.[6] Let us take these two issues in turn.

Those who wish to reject religion on the grounds that it undermines science must first explain how plenty of respectable scientists can hold orthodox religious views. Belief in God might not be common among contemporary scientists, but it is certainly

not an obstacle to scientific work. Many influential figures associated with the Enlightenment, starting with Francis Bacon, believed in the existence of God. Indeed, for many Enlightenment
figures including Isaac Newton himself, the elegant rules of the new
physics confirmed the existence of a legislating creator. Much has
been written about the atheism or otherwise of David Hume;
indeed, he is something of an idol for modern critics of religion. But
he was quite clear that religion and philosophy occupied separate
spheres; speaking of religion he once declared that 'The whole is a
riddle, an enigma, an inexplicable mystery. Doubt, uncertainty,
suspense of judgment appear the only result of our most accurate
scrutiny concerning the subject.' He was happy to make his escape
into 'the calm, though obscure, regions of philosophy'.[7] The
mainstream Christian churches, and many agnostic or atheist scientists, agree that there is no need for conflict between religious faith
and scientific reason. In November 2005 Cardinal Schoenborn, an
Austrian theologian close to the new pope, said that 'the biblical
teaching about creation is not a scientific theory . . . Christian
teaching about creation is not an alternative to evolution.'[8] The
evolutionary biologist and popular science writer Stephen Jay
Gould argued for a very similar point of view when he spoke of
'nonoverlapping magisteria'.[9]

It is not clear that one can object to religion on the grounds that it
has no rational basis without rejecting morality on the same
grounds. We do not need God in order to be moral, of course.
But if we are to act as moral agents, we need to believe that we are
bound by moral principles. Yet this belief cannot be denied from
reason alone. Sam Harris asserts that we must find 'approaches to
ethics and spiritual experience that make no appeal to faith, and
[broadcast] this knowledge to everyone'.[10] There is something
appealing about this idea, but he is clearly wrong to imagine that
we can move from the facts of the world to a moral commitment to
others without in some sense acting beyond reason. 'We are bound
to one another', he says, echoing generations of mystics, and most of
us, I hope, are inclined to agree.[11] But the decision to believe this is
not an inevitable consequence of rational analysis. We must in the

end decide for ourselves how we construe our moral duties to one another. It is fanciful to claim that a description of the world can somehow generate a morality.[12]

It follows that, insofar as our approach to Enlightenment itself entails moral claims, it cannot be understood without reference to beliefs that have no basis in reason. There is no more factual basis for the claim that we have a moral duty to discover and share the truth than there is for the claim that Jesus was the son of God. A scientist working on secret weapons research may be operating at a very high theoretical and technical level, but if they have no interest in how the research is used, they have no claim to be enlightened, except in the occult sense discussed in the previous chapter. Secrecy precludes Open Enlightenment, since Open Enlightenment insists on the primacy of truth over all other considerations. A researcher enlightened in this sense does not seek out the truth for themselves, or for their institution's, benefit; they seek the truth in order to add to the common store of knowledge. But this attitude *towards* scientific inquiry cannot itself be derived *from* scientific inquiry. One can be a good scientist and work in conditions of total secrecy.

And consider the researcher who discovers evidence that a widely used chemical is harmful. Perhaps they inform their superior and leave their boss to take any necessary steps. This might be in line with institutional protocols and their research in itself might have been impeccable. But Open Enlightenment demands that they act as best they can to warn their fellow citizens. In doing so they bear witness to the moral force of true description – a moral force that may or may not exist independently of themselves, but which they have decided to recognize. Reason alone cannot lead them to such an action. They must decide for truth on some basis other than the scientific method.

So orthodox religious beliefs are not of a relevantly different nature from the beliefs of someone who seeks to defend and promote the values of Enlightenment in the fullest sense of the word. It makes no sense to think, as the Chicago geneticist Jerry Coyne suggests, that 'the *real* war is between rationalism and superstition'[13]. The idea that one could be motivated solely by reason to defend reason is incoherent. Certainly there is no way that reason can cause us to believe in God, but neither can it cause us to believe that it is wrong to kill. Notice here that I am not arguing for the existence of God. Religious people might very well be wrong in detail and in general about their beliefs. We don't need God to understand the universe, nor do we need God in order to believe that it is good to understand and to share our understanding. But the conflict between the Enlightenment and its enemies cannot be reduced to a conflict between faith and reason. Both the religious convictions of many figures in the historical Enlightenment and the ability of contemporary scientists to think rationally while believing in God confirm this in fact. Whether we like it or not, there is room for the religious, and religion, in the Enlightenment tradition. An Enlightenment purged of the non-rational is a chimera. If it is good to know, and if we have a duty to truth, then Enlightenment does not escape from the realm of moral judgements.

Perhaps the pernicious consequences of religion justify its central position as an enemy of the Enlightenment. Of course, religion does sometimes clash with the Enlightenment tradition, especially when religion takes a fundamentalist form. Religion has certainly in the past provided both the motive and the justification for great crimes. The rise of the religious right is a matter of concern and the struggle against creationism is an important one. When the Catholic Church campaigns against the use of condoms to control the spread of AIDS we must surely resist it in the name of humanity and reasoned understanding. But if we want to resist tyrannical forms of religion effectively we must endeavour to understand religion itself as fully as possible, both in its own right, and in the context of its relationship with other forms of power. Perhaps fundamentalism, the belief in the literal truth of holy texts, must lead to conflict with reason.

In *The End of Faith* (2005) Sam Harris argues passionately for the need to reject biblical and Koranic literalism in order to create a peaceful world:

> It is imperative that we begin to speak plainly about the absurdity of most of our religious beliefs . . . I pray that we may one day

think clearly enough about these matters to render our children incapable of killing themselves over their books. If not our children, then I suspect it could well be too late for us, because while it has never been difficult to meet your maker, in fifty years it will simply be too easy to drag everyone else along to meet him with you.[14]

Harris takes religion in its full sense to be a collection of dogmatic and outdated claims about the nature of the universe that cause conflict between groups. Because Muslim and Christian holy texts denounce other religions, and fundamentalists say that they take these books literally, Harris concludes that 'religions are *intrinsically* hostile to one another'.[15] Their mutual hostility, combined with their expressed hatred of non-believers, make religions uniquely dangerous, according to Harris, as sources of violent conflict.

Harris quotes a particularly bloodthirsty passage from Deuteronomy to illustrate the thoroughgoing murderousness and intolerance of fundamentalist Christianity:

> If your very own brother, or your son or daughter, or the wife you love, or your closest friend secretly entices you, saying, 'Let us go and worship other gods' (gods that neither you nor your fathers have known, gods of the peoples around you, whether near or far, from one end of the land to the other), do not yield to him or listen to him. Show him no pity. Do not spare him or shield him. You must certainly put him to death. Your hand must be the first in putting him to death, and then the hands of all the people. Stone him to death, because he tried to turn you away from the Lord your God, who brought you out of Egypt, out of the land of slavery. Then all Israel will hear and be afraid, and no one among you will do such an evil thing again.[16]

As Harris points out, taken literally, this means that if your sister tries to persuade you to join her yoga class, you have to kill her. Fundamentalists don't, on the whole, go around killing people for advocating yoga. The Bible also forbids astrology:

When you enter the land the Lord your God is giving you, do not learn to imitate the detestable ways of the nations there. Let no one be found among you who sacrifices his son or daughter in the fire, who practises divination or sorcery, interprets omens, engages in witchcraft, or casts spells, or who is a medium or spiritist or who consults the dead. Anyone who does these things is detestable to the Lord, and because of these detestable practices the Lord your God will drive out those nations before you. You must be blameless before the Lord your God.[17]

Yet Ronald and Nancy Reagan regularly consulted astrologers in their time in the White House. This didn't stop the religious right from supporting him in 1988,[18] when they first learned of this blatant witchcraft, or from venerating him in the years after his departure from public office. The President could practise divination, even rely on it at crucial moments in his Presidency, without fear of serious criticism. No right-wing religious leader would denounce Nancy and Ronald Reagan, in public at any rate. Yet, if the Bible is inerrantly true, their practice of divination had serious implications for national security since it made the nation 'detestable to the Lord'.

Although fundamentalist Christians in the US and elsewhere claim to believe in the literal truth of the Bible, given that the Bible bristles with contradictions, they cannot possibly do so. In reality fundamentalists pick the bits of the Bible they find useful or comforting and ignore whatever is inconvenient. Accordingly, left-wing fundamentalists and right-wing fundamentalists disagree vigorously with each other on matters such as the ordination of women, the need to enforce strict codes governing sexual morality, and the political implications of the Gospels.[19] For some reason, almost all fundamentalist Christians pay no attention to the dietary prohibitions in Leviticus and Deuteronomy, while loudly insisting on the continued relevance of the ban on homosexuality. 'Literal' readings of the Bible depend decisively on the social and historical context in which they are made.

Religion has been in decline for 400 years in Europe, the world leader in demonstrations of murderous piety. Economic development and improved material conditions have tended to reduce the power of centralized religious authority. A well-educated and less threatened population can afford to take a more relaxed attitude to the demands of religious institutions. Since the war Europeans have secured greater economic independence and greater security from poverty, and this has led to a steady retreat by traditional religion that has not been accompanied by any great success by Evangelical sects. The evidence seems to suggest that the power of religion – its ability to influence political decision-making – declines with the development of effective state welfare programmes.

In parts of Latin America and Africa, Evangelical Christianity is undoubtedly on the rise. The American writer Mike Davis has argued that Evangelical religion, especially Pentecostal Christianity, has become the dominant ideological force in the world's slums and that left-wing movements in the poorest districts are being eclipsed by ecstatic religion. Given the unemployment and criminality of slums in the developing world, the absence of anything resembling a traditional working class and the ruthlessness of the established order, spiritual salvation must seem more likely than material progress. But before we cluck at the inveterate irrationality of the poor and steel ourselves for a renewed assault on superstition, we ought to recognize that the catastrophic urbanization of the last two decades in Africa and Latin America has come about as a result of development policies imposed by the World Bank and the IMF. These policies, conceived by self-declared successors to Adam Smith, have destroyed the purchasing power of rural communities and condemned hundreds of millions of economic migrants to desperation. The growth of the Pentecostal churches under these conditions is a perversely appropriate monument to structural readjustment and trade liberalization, the favoured policies of the enlightened elites responsible for policy in the global institutions.[20]

Roughly half of America's 160 million Protestants 'describe themselves as being born again'.[21] That is, they have chosen as adults to be baptized and to accept Jesus Christ as their saviour. This decision, and the accompanying commitment to persuade others to take baptism, define the Evangelical movement as a whole. The combined power of personal transformation and the associated mission to convert account for a great deal of this movement's power to mobilize the faithful and increase their numbers. But their shared experiences of God's wonder-working power – and their collective desire to share the good news – are all that unite Evangelicals as a matter of necessity. For the rest, one can talk sensibly about tendencies and styles – there are charismatics, dominionists, Baptists, Methodists and left-wing congregations. But it is important to stress that all that Evangelicals have in common is the shared sensation of being born again in Christ. There is no unified leadership structure, and no central body for enforcing orthodoxy; rather there are thousands of churches competing for the attention of the public in a highly competitive and lucrative market.

Evangelicals are growing in number and they have played an important role in maintaining the Republican ascendancy since 1968. In the 2004 election, 78 per cent of white Evangelicals voted for Bush, up from 68 per cent in 2000, and Bush's increased share of the Evangelical vote played a large part in securing his victory over Senator John Kerry. Still, there are signs that Evangelicals are becoming disenchanted. The Republican share of the white Evangelical vote in the mid-term elections of 2006 went down slightly to 71 per cent, and increased Evangelical support for Democrats was decisive in some close races.[22] More generally, the role of religion in American life is somewhat more ambiguous than one might think. For example, while around 85 per cent of all Americans claim to be Christians, only 40 per cent of them can name more than four of the Ten Commandments.[23] When Christmas Day fell on a Sunday in 2005, many Evangelical pastors did not expect the faithful to turn up at church. They recognized that Christmas was 'family time' for a country that has far fewer holidays than other Western nations. More seriously, the scandals that engulfed Evangelical leaders in both 1988 and 2006 show how reliably vulnerable they are to accusations of moral hypocrisy. And while no politician could get away with open atheism, no politician could be so devout as to disparage another religion. America still runs on Eisenhower's stated principle, 'Our government makes no sense unless it is founded on a deeply felt religious faith – and I don't care what it is.'[24]

Even after 9/11 and the subsequent invasions of Afghanistan and Iraq in 2001 and 2003 respectively, it is still far from obvious that contemporary world history is best understood in religious terms. Indeed it is not clear that 'religion', unalloyed with other cultural and material considerations, provides an adequate explanation for much of anything at all. Doubtless as and when China and Russia again engross America's defence intellectuals, religion will once again recede as a useful explanatory mechanism and the idea of 'a clash of civilizations' will be refurbished on different lines.

Modern religion is entangled with other forms of power in ways that would repay further study. Let us look more closely at this entanglement of faith and domination in the United States. After all, if it is the tyrannical aspect of religion that concerns us, then we must be very careful not to focus on the details of faith to the point where we ignore or underestimate other forms of illegitimate power.

RELIGION AND AMERICAN POWER

The spectacular rise and fall of Washington lobbyist Jack Abramoff allows us an insight into the way in which religion interacts with other interests in the United States at the present time. A former head of the College Republican National Committee, Abramoff made millions representing Native American tribal casinos. In 2001 he persuaded the Louisiana Coushatta tribe that it faced possible competition over the border in Texas. In a memo to the Coushatta, Abramoff's associate Michael Scanlon explained how a targeted media campaign would mobilize opposition to any expansion of gambling in Texas:

> Our mission is to get specifically selected groups of individuals to the polls to speak out AGAINST something . . . To that end, your money is best spent finding them and communicating with

them on using the modes that they are most likely to respond to. Simply put we want to bring out the wackos to vote against something and make sure the rest of the public lets the whole thing slip past them. The wackos get their information form [sic] the Christian right, Christian radio, mail, the internet and telephone trees.[25]

In other words, Abramoff and Scanlon mobilized Evangelical opponents of gambling in Texas to ensure that their clients across the border in Louisiana wouldn't face competition. In this campaign and others, Abramoff and Scanlon worked with the former executive director of the Christian Coalition, Ralph Reed. In October 2001 Reed claimed that he had '50 pastors mobilized, with a total membership in those churches of over 40,000' as part of the campaign against gambling in Texas.[26] A few months later he told Abramoff that he had secured the support of prominent Evangelicals Jim Dobson, Gary Bauer, Jerry Falwell and Pat Robertson for the campaign. Presumably this was all part of Abramoff and Scanlon's attempts to 'bring out the wackos'. The 2001 grass-roots campaign was only one of many expensive operations that Scanlon and Abramoff sold to the Coushatta Indians. In all, Scanlon billed them for some $30 million for PR work and secretly passed about $11.5 million on to his partner Abramoff.[27]

The two men deceived and exploited other Indian tribes. In another case, Abramoff worked with the authorities in Texas to close down a casino operated by the Tigua tribe. He then approached the hapless casino-owners and offered his services. His only condition was that they take on Scanlon's public relations firm. The two men then split the proceeds from Scanlon's greatly inflated fees. They called these scams 'Gimme Five'.[28] In all, Scanlon and Abramoff shared the profits from $66 million in fees that Scanlon charged to his clients in the years 2001–3.[29] As one considers their career, its double-dealing and its conscious regimentation of popular outrage, it is difficult not to think of Julien Benda's complaint in *La Trahison des Clercs* (1927): 'our age is indeed the age of the intellectual organization of political hatreds'.[30]

As a staunch Evangelical, Reed couldn't take money directly from gambling interests, so Abramoff and Scanlon arranged for him to be paid through third parties, including an organization run by Grover Norquist called Citizens for Tax Reform. Newt Gingrich once said that Norquist was 'the person I regard as the most innovative, creative, courageous and entrepreneurial leader of the anti-tax efforts and of conservative grassroots activism in America'. The entrepreneurial part is accurate – Scanlon and Abramoff's emails record their astonishment at the way Norquist siphoned off money intended for Reed, almost as though he was imposing a tax. Reed and Robertson and the other Evangelicals might have been unwitting dupes in all this of course, but at least Reed got some sort of compensation for his time – a little more than $4 million according to the *Washington Post*.[31]

The antics of Jack Abramoff and his associates provide a well-documented example of the way in which the religious right interacts with other sources of power in the US. Clients pay vast sums to lobbyists and political consultants, who then excite the moral indignation of 'wackos'. Some of the money finds its way to legislators in the form of expensive trips and other benefits. Deniability is maintained through cut-out organizations where necessary; front companies, pressure groups and so on. In all of this, the Evangelical rank and file are a long way down the food chain. Abramoff and Scanlon were unusually greedy and reckless, but their methods can be seen repeated on a much larger scale, albeit with somewhat greater discretion, in America's national politics.

Financial forces and religious sentiment combine in the creation of the right-wing Evangelical media in the United States. In the early days of broadcasting, federal rules had stipulated that television networks made a certain amount of time available for 'public interest programming'. In practice this was mostly provided by religious groups. At first the networks had given this 'public interest' airtime away for free. But in 1960 the Federal Communications Commission allowed broadcasters to sell airtime to religious groups. They also exempted these programmes from the rules limiting the

number of commercials per hour elsewhere on the schedules. As John Stauber and Sheldon Rampton point out in their book *Banana Republicans* (2004), 'TV stations quickly realised that they could maximise their profits by offering airtime to paying religious broadcasters, which in turn favoured a specific *type* of religious broadcaster'.[32] Evangelical preachers, who tended to come from the South and tended to be right-wing, were already well versed in fund-raising through appeals to the faithful, and they could see the entrepreneurial possibilities of regular access to a mass audience. The televangelists 'brought the carnival-like showmanship of revivalist tent shows to television religion'.[33] The Evangelicals were only too willing to raise money from broadcasting in a way that other Christian groups, including more liberal sects, found alien.

On only a cursory inspection, it is clear that right-wing religion is closely integrated by the profit motive with political power in the United States. To pull at only one other thread, in 1997 Karl Rove secured Jack Abramoff's associate, Ralph Reed, a job as a consultant for Enron, for which he received between $10,000 and $20,000 per month in the years before that company's spectacular collapse. Enron was being used as a vehicle to buy the support of Evangelicals for Bush in the 2000 election, especially in the run-up to the Republican primaries, when Evangelical voters were at their most influential. Members of the Evangelical leadership were being paid by Enron, an essentially criminal entity, at the behest of Karl Rove. This must call into question their fulsome praise for Bush. It must also qualify the sense in which the religious right is properly speaking a religious phenomenon at all. In light of what we know, it looks much more like a protection racket. The suspicion that support from the religious is a commodity sold by its leadership receives a certain amount of confirmation from Bush's own religious status. For all that he lards his speeches with religious terms that resonate with the Evangelical rank and file, Bush has never openly declared that he has been born again. Given that sharing the good news of rebirth in Christ is about the only thing that defines a Evangelical Christian, he makes a funny kind of role model for th sincerely religious.

When it isn't taking money from corrupt corporations and lobbyists, the religious right agitates tirelessly for the abolition of the inevitable. The 'solutions' they propose – sexual abstinence as contraception, 'cures' for homosexuality, an unrelenting war on drugs – aren't really the point of their activity. The solutions would be unworkable or disastrous if they were ever put into practice. The point is not to ban gambling, abortion or homosexual marriage. The point for leaders of the religious right is to keep such irrelevancies at the centre of political debate and so to maintain an atmosphere of ongoing moral emergency. It is in this that the power of the religious right's leadership has resided over the last twenty-five years. The key asset they control is the obedience of their followers. Their claim to control millions of votes allows them to charge politicians for their public support.[34]

Brokered in this way, faith, in the words of Theodor W. Adorno and Max Horkheimer, 'degenerates into a swindle'[35] – a means to power and wealth for some Evangelical leaders of course, but more importantly a method by which elites in business and government can pursue their goals without having to concede – or reveal – too much to the wider public. Far from posing an independent 'threat to reason', right-wing religion is a junior partner in a coalition dominated by the interests of others. To a degree that is almost comical, the right-wing Evangelicals unerringly side with the most powerful forces in society. On matters of taxation and economic policy they enthusiastically echo the demands of the rich.[36] In foreign policy, they were happy to provide biblical corroboration for the need to invade Iraq, or Babylon as they preferred to call it, and they have revised their traditional anti-Semitism to give un-wavering support to Israel. This support has a peculiar quality, of course, since these Evangelicals cheerfully expect the Jews to be annihilated in Armageddon.[37]

If we ignore the context in which right-wing religion operates in the United States and focus exclusively on the differences between Evangelicals and secular liberals, we will unwittingly find ourselves incorporated into a far larger and deeper system of deception, in which fraudulent religion plays only a part. The leadership of the

religious right would like nothing more than to present its activities in terms of a showdown with the values of the Enlightenment, since this will increase its hold on its followers. Liberal intellectuals help the Evangelical right by taking their theological extravagance seriously and by treating them as a movement of world-historical significance. In this process the prestige of the Enlightenment is deployed to disastrous effect. Instead of treating right-wing religion as a human phenomenon with identifiable strategies, strengths and weaknesses, the defenders of the Enlightenment insist that it is a central, perhaps *the* central, threat to reason.

HOW DO YOU SOLVE A PROBLEM LIKE TYRANNICAL RELIGION?

Now faith is the conviction of things hoped for, the assurance of things not seen.

Hebrews, 11: 1

All this is not to downplay the dangers inherent in faith-based politics. But if we want to resist the tyrannical aspect of the religious right we have two alternatives. Either we can declare war on religious irrationality and try to break the power of the religious right indirectly by depriving them of their congregations; or we can challenge them directly by establishing in greater detail how they operate and by sharing that information with their followers. In other words, we can either engage in an essentially theological dispute with millions of devout Christians, both moderate and fundamentalist, or we can try to show how Evangelicals have been manipulated by a leadership that sees them as a resource to be sold to politicians. This latter course requires that we work much harder as citizens to understand the mechanics of electoral politics in the United States than we do at present. It also requires secular intellectuals to take the psychology of religious experience much more seriously. The experience and effects of being born again in particular must be better understood if we are serious about saving the faithful from exploitation. No powerful institutional interests would be served by such programmes of inquiry. The media welcomes the drama of the conflict between Evangelical conservatives and secular liberals. As an entertainment genre it is more compelling than, say, discussions of social justice, which come down in the end to quarrels about graphs and who gets what; much better to stage a heated argument about the soul of the Republic.

We can also see how matters of pressing concern to progressives might be framed in terms that engage the Evangelical imagination. For example, the large, publicly traded corporations are a source of great anxiety for those who seek a more just society, and these corporations have some very thought-provoking characteristics. The academic and lawyer Joel Bakan explains:

> Corporations are created by law and imbued with purpose by law. Law dictates what their directors and managers can do, what they cannot do, and what they must do. At least in the United States and other industrialized countries, the corporation, as created by law . . . compels executives to prioritize the interests of their companies and shareholders above all others and forbids them from being socially responsible – at least genuinely so.[38]

As persons created in law, corporations do not age and have no natural term to their activities. In 1929 the Georgia Supreme Court explained that 'freed, as such bodies are, from the sure bounds to the schemes of individuals – the grave – they are able to add field to field, and power to power, until they become entirely too strong for that society which is made up of those whose plans are limited to a single life.'[39] They are, as a matter of legal necessity, indifferent to the consequences of their actions, except insofar as they concern the interests of their shareholders; they are highly manipulative in their dealings with everyone but their owners, since they must constantly deny or disguise their nature by presenting themselves as socially responsible actors.[40]

This inhuman clarity of purpose, to elevate the interests of their shareholders above all other considerations, can be understood in terms of mental illness. Bakan demonstrates convincingly that if we look steadily at its institutional character, we must recognize that the corporation can plausibly be described as psychopathic.[41] Christians, especially Evangelical Christians, might prefer to use the word 'demonic'. The corporation is a fictitious person, a person called into being by law; it is incapable of serving anything but the interests of those who own it, and it is given both form and substance by the human beings that work for it. The publicly traded corporations are, as a matter of legal necessity, monsters: in themselves 'they have neither bodies to be punished, nor souls to be condemned; they therefore do as they like.'[42] To respond to the facts of their institutional nature, as one would-be enlightened critic of fundamentalism does, by declaring that 'I reject the view of the conspiracy theorists that all multinational companies sacrifice all ethical considerations for the sake of profit'[43] is to exhibit an almost childlike faith in the sincerity of corporate press releases; it is nothing if not the conviction of things hoped for, the assurance of things not seen.

The Evangelicals wish to fight monsters and to create a world free of sin. Let us invite them to join us in a crusade against these demonic concentrations of greed – for what is a thing that does not live and does not age, that can only treat others as resources to be used and discarded? The moral abomination presented by the modern industrial corporation must appeal to the Evangelical imagination more strongly than the timid managerialism of the Democrats and the modern British Labour Party. It is in this that we can find the means to break the enchantment of 'the great divide' between faith and reason and replace it with a broad-based and uncompromising movement to understand and then transform the world.

The Abramoff scandal provides a useful way of appreciating how religion operates in partnership with other forms of power in the United States. And the United States itself helps us to understand religion in a global context. Any attempt to think about religion in isolation from other factors will lead to catastrophic misunderstanding. The rise of fundamentalist Christianity in Latin America and of fundamentalist Islam in the Middle East have taken place under particular economic, political and cultural conditions. We might not be able to understand exactly how these forces combine, but we can recognize that they do so. There is no need to fantasize about converting the faithful from beliefs that give meaning to their lives, beliefs that are, in Karl Marx's words, 'the heart of a heartless world'. We need only reveal to them the true nature of the leadership that beguiles them and sells their sincere desire for a better world to the servants of a diabolical system of fair-seeming villainy.

If we are to resist the tyrannical expressions of religion, we have to stop believing that hostility to religion suffices to make us enlightened. Indeed uncompromising hostility to religion, however pleasurable, will only isolate intellectuals from the rest of society, especially in America. Further, we need to recognize how hostility to religion leaves intact much more serious threats to reason. Properly understood, Enlightenment turns out to promise us a very worldly kind of discomfort – the very opposite of the cosy theological musings of Dawkins and Harris.

5

The Threat to Science

Oh, how much is today hidden by science! Oh, how much it is expected to hide!

Friedrich Nietzsche, *The Genealogy of Morals* (1887)

Enlightenment, in the sense of a moral commitment to truth, cannot be reached by reason alone. To decide for truth is to step beyond the operations of reason. The Folk Enlightenment, in which reason and faith are separated by a 'great divide', cannot be justified if it is based on a simple-minded distinction between the rational and the irrational. We must therefore think much more carefully about what are usually presented as the 'irrational' threats to reason. If our response to them is to be enlightened, it must be proportionate to the threat they pose to open inquiry and to the unprejudiced pursuit of knowledge. It must also be informed by an understanding of their relationship with other forms of power and their significance relative to those forms of power.

Modern science is rightly hailed as the great achievement of the Age of Enlightenment. If it makes sense to talk of what we have inherited from that era, it does so above all in the context of science. But we must be clear that science can be enlightened in two senses. Science can be conducted openly, in the service of humanity, or it can be conducted in secrecy, in pursuit of institutional advantage. Science that exclusively serves institutional interests cannot claim to be enlightened in anything other than the occult sense. Science is enlightened in the full and open sense insofar as it contributes to human welfare. Whatever threatens this form of science must be resisted by those who wish to aid humanity. If the irrational enemies of science constitute the greatest threat to science in this sense of open and free inquiry, then perhaps here we can reconvene the great confrontation between reason and unreason that informs the Folk Enlightenment. But if open and free inquiry faces a more serious threat from institutions that are themselves closely associated with science and are themselves normally considered enlightened, we face a threat that is more potentially confusing.

According to writers who want to retain the formal structure of the Folk Enlightenment, the main threats to science come from fundamentalists who reject evolution, radical environmentalists who believe that 'humans are literally a species out of control',[1] anti-humanists who reject the possibility of material progress, and advocates of alternative and holistic forms of medicine. Frank Furedi, the British intellectual, claims that traditional forms of authority, including scientific authority, have collapsed and a host of gurus, therapists and mentors have flocked to take their place. The public itself has become a menace to science:

> We are suspicious of medical doctors but we feel comfortable with healers who mumble on about being 'holistic' and 'natural'. We certainly don't trust scientists working for the pharmaceutical industry but we are happy to listen to the disinterested opinion of a herbalist. And, of course, alternative food and other consumer products gain our confidence because . . . they are alternative.[2]

In his evocatively titled *The March of Unreason* (2005), Dick Taverne tries to argue that 'alternative medicine, proponents of organic farming, anti-GM protestors' and what he describes as 'eco-fundamentalists'[3] pose a significant threat to enlightened science: '[These] reactions against science and technology . . . mainly reflect a general instinctive malaise – that natural remedies and natural farming methods are best, that we are losing touch with nature, and that science is subjecting us to ever greater risks of harm.'[4] Those who object to GM crops, distrust conventional medicine, or advocate organic farming don't use reasonable arguments, according to Taverne; they just *feel* there is something wrong with modern civilization, with human nature itself. Similarly, the Social Issues Research Centre, a think tank based in Oxford, declares that 'rational debate about food safety and quality has been replaced by irrational scaremongering.'[5]

When Taverne writes about the 'market power' that has protected herbalists from 'effective and necessary regulation'[6] it takes a moment to realize that he is being serious. Let us look at alternative medicine and compare it with the current system found in conventional medicine. If alternative therapists really do threaten the enlightened inheritance more than elements within conventional medicine, then the Folk Enlightenment might also start to become more plausible. But if the most serious enemies of science are not irrational, if indeed they loudly insist that they are science's greatest allies, then the clash between the rational and the irrational can no longer be central to our intellectual and moral concerns in this context. I do not have the space to look beyond medical science, but it will serve our purposes. For as medical science is, or should be, a matter of alleviating human suffering, it is, or should be, the very epitome of enlightened progress.

Alternative medicine is a big and sinister business, according to its critics. It is certainly true that it can be sinister. Plenty of old-school quacks and snake-oil salesmen are peddling their miracle cures for terminal cancer. They are aided by the credulity and good intentions of the general public, and they prey on the desperation of those whom conventional medicine cannot help. They employ great ingenuity in their frauds and they enthusiastically abuse scientific language. They sell empty hope to the hopeless and they are, of course, despicable.

Aside from the last-chance miracle cures for cancer, many of the herbal pills and potions sold in health food shops work no better than a placebo, a sugar pill. In 2003 Americans spent $4.4 billion on these kinds of medicine. This sounds like a lot of money until you look at the sums spent on conventional healthcare. In the United

States total spending on health in the same year accounted for 15 per cent of total GDP – something like $1,640 billion. Spending on conventional pharmaceutical medicine accounted for some $211 billion – nearly fifty times more than was spent on herbs and homeopathic potions.[7] And while alternative therapies do cause some deaths and illness, the damage doesn't appear to be vast. A visit to the homeopath might mean we delay seeking medical advice from someone with conventional medical expertise, but distilled water with the 'memory' of a now non-existent chemical is not the stuff that overdoses are made of. Herbal medicines, especially in combination with conventional drugs, can be dangerous, but again the casualty rate is quite low. The World Health Organization recorded 8,985 'adverse events associated with herbal medicines' world-wide between 1968 and 1997.[8]

Meanwhile in 1998 a University of Toronto research team estimated that 106,000 Americans die every year from the side effects of 'appropriately administered, FDA-approved drugs'. Some of these deaths were doubtless unavoidable – a life-saving drug might have eventually fatal side effects. But a trade-off between real risks and benefits might not account for many, even most, of these drug-related fatalities. CNN quoted one of the team explaining, 'We're not saying, "Don't take drugs." They have wonderful benefits. But what we're arguing is that there should be increased awareness also of side effects, which until now have not been too well understood.'[9] Given that pharmaceutical medicine is fifty times more lucrative, and considerably more lethal, than the herbal and homeopathic alternatives, the institutions that control the business might be suspected of posing a greater threat to reason than their reiki-practising competitors. And as we shall see, these institutions do indeed undermine the open, humane science they claim to champion in two key ways. Firstly they demonstrably corrupt the conduct of science: they withhold information, they present information to the public in misleading ways, they threaten scientists who make inconvenient discoveries and they punish those who inform the public about those discoveries. Secondly, and more pervasively, they distract attention from forms of healthcare that do not conform to their business model, the exploitation of lucrative patents.

Let's start by looking at the ways that the dominant institutions in this sector directly undermine good scientific conduct. A new drug can only enter the market if regulators are satisfied that it is effective and safe. But companies like to use young patients in trials, which reduces the chances that harmful side effects will be discovered, even though most drugs are used by older people. They also test over short periods of time, which again makes it less likely that problems will be identified before a drug is approved. Furthermore, a new drug does not need to be shown to be more effective than treatments that are already available. Drug companies regularly test new medicines against a placebo rather than against existing treatments, so regulators and doctors can have no idea if the new medicines represent a genuine advance, or whether they are in fact less effective than an older, perhaps cheaper, drug. When the companies do test against older drugs, they sometimes use inappropriate dosages, so that the new, more expensive drugs appear to be more effective. The heartburn treatment Nexium was presented as an improvement on Prilosec in this way.[10]

Regulators have recently approved drugs that are much more dangerous than existing treatments. In extreme cases they have approved drugs with lethal side effects and allowed them to remain widely available for years after evidence of a major problem had emerged, as we shall see. In order to bypass the regulators, companies sometimes suppress trials that don't show the desired results and publish the ones that do. For example, the psychiatrist David Healy has described how the multinational GSK conducted 'nine studies of Paxil, a drug used to treat depression and anxiety, in children and adolescents, eight of which were unpublished. When the British regulators got to see all these studies in June 2003, they concluded that, combined, they pointed to a 1.5 to 3.2 times greater risk of suicidality on Paxil than on placebo'.[11]

The selective serotonin uptake inhibitors (SSRIs), of which Paxil is one, constitute one of the great business success stories of the last two decades. Launched commercially in 1988 in the USA and

Canada, Eli Lilly's Prozac became one of the most popular drugs of all time. By 2004 it had been prescribed to more than 50 million people. In the same year antidepressants in the United States generated more than $10 billion in sales. Though the actual advantages of SSRIs over older, cheaper antidepressants didn't amount to a huge amount (they had a slightly improved side-effect profile – no more cotton mouth – and dosing was more straightforward), this didn't stop their supporters from talking about miracles.[12] These drugs wouldn't just help the mentally ill; everyone's lives could be improved. Better living through chemicals really was possible.

The arrival of new drugs protected by patent coincided with 'a thousandfold increase in the diagnosis of depression'.[13] Doubtless some of these people had been suffering in silence before Prozac arrived, but even the most determined defender of the therapeutic status quo would have a hard time arguing that this increase in the diagnosis of depression had nothing to do with the energetic marketing efforts of the drug companies. Furthermore, claims that the new drugs didn't cause dependence proved excessively optimistic. If anything they caused more problems in this respect than the benzodiazepines they replaced.[14] The new drugs had an added disadvantage: as David Healy writes in *Let Them Eat Prozac* (2005), 'SSRIs trigger suicidality in a significant proportion of those who take them'.[15] As early as 1986, Eli Lilly's own figures suggested that the 'rates of suicide attempts were three to four times higher on Prozac than either on other antidepressants or on placebo'.[16]

Perhaps the drug that has caused the most harm to the public in recent years is Vioxx. Marketed as an alternative to non-steroidal anti-inflammatory drugs (NSAIDs) such as paracetamol, aspirin and ibuprofen, Vioxx had an important advantage over those older drugs: it didn't cause intestinal bleeding. In testimony to the US Senate Finance Committee in 2004, Gurkirpal Singh, an adjunct professor of medicine at Stanford University, explained:

> There are two enzymes in the body – cox-1 and cox-2 . . . Cox-1 enzyme is needed for the normal functioning of stomach and

platelets. Cox-2 enzyme, on the other hand, is thought to be responsible for pain and swelling of arthritis. Traditional pain-killers such as ibuprofen . . . inhibit both cox-1 and cox-2. This means that while these drugs are effective in reducing pain, they increase the risk of stomach bleeding. A few years ago, my colleagues and I estimated that there are over 103,000 hospitalizations and 16,500 deaths every year from the stomach bleeding complications of these drugs . . . The specific cox-2 inhibitors such as Vioxx and Celebrex were developed to inhibit only cox-2, and not cox-1. It was hoped that these drugs would relieve pain but not have any stomach problems.[17]

These new drugs were painkillers. They did not cure arthritis or any other diseases. They reduced the risk of stomach bleeding, but only marginally more than a combination of older drugs did. According to Singh, 'a combination of two older drugs – a pain-relieving drug such as motrin [i.e. ibuprofen] with a drug that protects the stomach such as prilosec – is as effective and almost as safe on the stomach as Vioxx, with no heart attack risk'. In his testimony Singh was at pains to emphasize that 'there are many other ways to control pain as well'. But by destroying the cox–1 enzyme, aspirin 'prevents blood from clotting in the heart blood vessels, thus helping reduce the risk of heart attacks'. Cox-2 inhibitors had no such effect on the risk of heart attacks. This immediately spelled trouble for the company developing Vioxx. Singh's testimony continues:

By 1999 an even more serious problem was emerging. By the time Merck had filed for the approval of Vioxx, there were several small studies evaluating the efficacy and safety of Vioxx in patients with pain and arthritis. None of these studies were large enough to study the risk-benefit trade-offs of stomach bleeds versus heart attacks. But a careful FDA review of the Merck's new drug application for Vioxx showed that 'thromboembolic events [such as heart attack and stroke] are more frequent in patients receiving Vioxx than placebo . . .'

Singh goes on to explain that 'this means that not only did Vioxx not inhibit the platelets, but for some reason, it was likely to promote heart attacks directly.' Despite what looked like clear grounds for further precautionary research, the Food and Drug Administration (FDA) approved the drug for release in May 1999, after a 'priority review'.[18]

In his testimony at the same Senate hearing in 2004, David Graham, the Associate Director of Science and Medicine in the Office of Drug Safety in the FDA, revealed that there had been even more evidence that pointed to the need for further study, at the very least: 'Prior to approval of Vioxx, a study was performed by Merck called 090. This study found nearly a 7-fold increase in heart attack risk with low dose Vioxx.'[19] In March 2000, more data arrived that indicated a problem with Vioxx.[20] Early results from an industry-sponsored trial called VIGOR appeared to show 'a 500% increase in heart attacks with Vioxx'.[21] At this point, Graham argues that the FDA should have banned high-dose Vioxx.[22] Had they done so, many thousands of lives would have been saved. Instead, more than a year later Merck was still circulating press releases that claimed Vioxx had a 'favorable cardiovascular safety profile'.[23] The drug remained widely used for more than four years after the VIGOR trial.

In commercial terms Vioxx was highly successful. By 2000, annual sales of the drug approached $1.5 billion. In that year Merck made Vioxx the most heavily advertised drug in the United States. The $160 million advertising budget comfortably exceeded the amount spent advertising Pepsi in the same period. David Graham is in no doubt that this advertising had a huge impact on the popularity of Vioxx: 'Direct-to-consumer advertising is part of what made Vioxx a blockbuster drug. It helped to rev the market up to get people to want to use the drug'.[24] At last, on 25 August 2004, a report from the FDA's Office of Drug Safety presented clear evidence of a major heart attack risk from Vioxx. Just over a month later, Merck voluntarily withdrew the drug from the USA and eighty other countries.[25]

The widespread use of the drug translated into a very large number of heart attacks and strokes, many of which were fatal.

David Graham, who co-authored the 2004 report, estimated that between 88,000 and 139,000 Americans had heart attacks or strokes as a result of taking Vioxx and that between 26,000 and 55,000 of them probably died.[26] Dr Eric Topol, at the time a professor of medicine at the Cleveland Clinic, put the likely number of heart attacks and strokes at 160,000.[27] To give some idea of the scale of the disaster, Graham pointed out that the number of people having heart attacks as a result of taking Vioxx was equivalent to the number of passengers on between 500 and 900 Boeing 747s – a major air crash or two every week for five years.[28] The drug that caused this spectacular number of heart attacks did not cure any disease, and had an only very slightly improved risk profile as regards stomach bleeding than a combination of ibuprofen and Prilosec. There had been evidence suggesting that Vioxx presented an unacceptable risk before its launch in 1999, and by mid-2000 there was little room left for doubt.

The response of the FDA's management to its own 2004 report revealed the likely consequences for scientists that act to protect the public interest. David Graham explained to the Senate Committee that:

> I was pressured to change my conclusions and recommendations, and basically threatened that if I did not change them, I would not be permitted to present the paper at the [International Conference on Pharmacoepidemiology, in Bordeaux, France] . . . In mid-August, despite our study showing an increased risk of heart attack with Vioxx, and despite the results of other studies published in the literature, FDA announced it had approved Vioxx for use in children with rheumatoid arthritis. Also, on September 22 . . . a senior manager from [the Office of Drug Safety] labelled our Vioxx study a 'scientific rumor'. Eight days later, Merck pulled Vioxx from the market, and jetliners stopped dropping from the sky.[29]

After the publication of the 2004 report, the FDA's senior management tried to minimize the public impact of Graham's findings and to discredit him personally. Allegations of scientific misconduct were made to the editor of the *Lancet* and to the United States' Government Accountability Project. The FDA also tried to prevent him from giving testimony to the Senate Finance Committee and offered him a new job, 'which basically would have been exile to a fancy title with no real ability to have an impact'.[30]

Between the emergence of a clear link between Vioxx and increased heart attack risks, tens of thousands of people died, many of them unnecessarily. Not only that, but once the drug was removed, the FDA worked hard to discredit its own employee in the eyes of the media and the Senate. This can hardly reassure us that the regulatory system for conventional medicine works tolerably well to protect the public. David Graham himself insists that we can't dismiss Vioxx as an unfortunate lapse in an otherwise adequate system. 'Vioxx is a terrible tragedy and a profound regulatory failure. I would argue that the FDA, as currently configured, is incapable of protecting America against another Vioxx. We are virtually defenceless.'[31] No amount of soothing talk about risk management and the price of progress should distract us from Graham's warnings. Instead we should surely take seriously his claim that the world's most important medical regulators 'the FDA and its Center for Drug Evaluation and Research are broken'.[32] While we should take no one person's word on trust, Graham's claims seem quite plausible, given his expertise, his first-hand experience, and the number of casualties caused by regulatory failure.

The Vioxx disaster indicates that the most serious threats to science in the public interest do not necessarily come from its irrational enemies. Attempts to intimidate or discredit scientists whose informed view is commercially inconvenient must surely qualify as a 'threat to reason'. When these attempts take place against a background of tens of thousands of unnecessary deaths, there are pressing practical as well as intellectual reasons to take them more seriously than the antics of shark cartilage salesmen and homeopaths. But Vioxx does not fit into the structure of the Folk Enlightenment: the system in which the disaster unfolded is not simply irrational. Indeed, the states and corporations that manage this system have a strong, albeit problematic, claim to the enlightened inheritance. But these institutions have always subordinated Enlightenment to their necessarily secret and often deceptive efforts to maximize profits and extend their power.

David Graham's efforts to stop the unnecessary deaths caused by Vioxx present a further problem for those writers who want to maintain the conflict between science and faith at the centre of Enlightenment language. In an interview in 2005, Graham was asked whether his Catholic faith played a part in his decision to risk his career:

It did in so far as my faith forms my conscience. It's sort of my sense of what's right and wrong and what I am and am not responsible for. I was in a situation with Vioxx where I was invited by Senator Grassley's office to testify. I could have told them no, but then they would have subpoenaed me. So of course I went peaceably. I was faced with this dilemma. Should I lay it on the line and tell them the way it really is or do I kind of downplay it? There are ways of doing that. What I concluded was that I'm now being given the opportunity to tell the truth to the people who are in a position to actually make a difference. I can't make a difference. I can't change the FDA, but Congress can. If I don't tell them the truth, then I'm now responsible, in part, for future deaths. I don't want to become a co-conspirator with the FDA in what happens with Vioxx because tens of thousands of people were injured or killed because of the FDA's disregard for safety. If I keep quiet about that, now I'm part of the problem. I'm one of them, and at that point then my conscience asks me, 'You know what the truth is, are you going to speak it or aren't you?'[33]

Aside from specific threats to science in the public interest that the Vioxx case reveals, there is another, more diffuse, but perhaps even more serious, problem with the current system. Research into disease conducted by corporations tends to favour lines of inquiry that offer the prospect of valuable patents. From a business perspective the ideal drug is one that can be sold at high prices to large numbers of affluent patients for long periods of time. In such circumstances it makes no sense to assume that pharmaceutical corporations can be left to decide on the research agenda. They can have little interest in researching and promoting forms of healthcare that promise few rewards for their shareholders.

Corporations justify the high prices they charge on the grounds that they need the money for research. But they concentrate on looking for patentable chemical compounds with which to manage diseases and lifestyle complaints in the developed world. Between 1970 and 1999, 1,400 new drugs were developed; of these only thirteen, fewer than one in a hundred, targeted tropical diseases. In 2000 there were no new drugs for tuberculosis, compared with eight for male sexual dysfunction and seven for baldness.[34] This balance of concerns reflects the commercial needs of the corporations and demonstrates the extent of their near-monopoly control over the content of research. Their massive market power and their equally massive public relations budget cannot help but influence academic researchers and government scientists. State-funded research largely conforms to the priorities of the corporations, and science education itself has to some extent been shaped by the needs of private industry. The new treatments that emerge from corporate-controlled medicine do not reflect any humane order of priorities and the public subsidies that contribute to this situation must surely be reviewed as a matter of urgency.

While the corporations are uninterested in the diseases of the poor, they are also uninterested in non-pharmaceutical forms of treatment. In the 1960s, experts were exploring the role of blood homocysteine and blood lipid levels in causing heart attacks. David Healy explains:

> The homocysteine hypothesis suggested a range of dietary approaches that might help, such as taking folate or B vitamins. The lipid-lowering approach gave rise to a generation of patented drugs aimed at lowering lipid levels, which became the

most profitable agents ever made. Rival evidence for homo-cysteine was effectively buried for almost thirty years.[35]

Isolated, albeit properly conducted, trials that seem to demonstrate the therapeutic benefits of non-pharmaceutical approaches are not automatically accepted into 'orthodox medicine', especially when they threaten lucrative markets for pharmaceutical drugs. Nor do they reliably lead to further research. At best they can hope for slow acceptance by a medical profession overloaded with data from pharmaceutical companies and wary of 'alternative' claims. At worst, promising new research in public health will be ignored or even dismissed out of hand.

In November 2004 the BBC reported on a University of Southern California study that suggested a link between poor diet in early childhood and antisocial behaviour later in life:

> The team took into account factors such as social background, health and education, the *American Journal of Psychiatry* reported. Report co-author Adrian Raine said parents could prevent their children developing bad behaviour by ensuring they got better diets. 'Poor nutrition leads to low IQ, which leads to later anti-social behaviour. At a societal level, should parents be thinking more about what kids are eating? There's more to anti-social behaviour than nutrition, but we argue that it is an important missing link.' . . . The researchers analysed the development of more than 1,000 children on Mauritius, an island in the Indian Ocean off the coast of Africa over 14 years. They found the more malnourished the children were, the greater the anti-social behaviour later on.[36]

The results of a double-blind trial against placebo conducted at a young offenders' institute in Aylesbury in the United Kingdom also indicated that an improved diet could lead to a significant reduction in violence among prison inmates. Speaking of the few trials that have taken place so far and the growing body of anecdotal evidence, the Oxford physiologist John Stein has said that 'it all calls out for a large, properly designed trial, but people won't stump up the money because you can't patent nutrition.'[37]

Faced with the results of the University of Southern California's fourteen-year study, Dr Ann Hagell, an advisor at the Nuffield Institute, said she 'would not dismiss the study out of hand', but that she 'would be surprised if diet played a big role':

> In my experience diet is not part of the explanation. It can cause hyper-activity disorders, but anti-social behaviour is more influenced by parenting and genetics and teen peer pressure in teenage groups.[38]

Perhaps another study should be conducted with a larger population group over a longer period of time, in which proper double-blind protocols are observed. In another twenty years or so we might have enough evidence to support the idea that good nutrition can contribute to a happy and healthy life. Or we can pay pharmaceutical companies to develop novel psychiatric drugs to give to mentally ill people who also happen, quite coincidentally, to be chronically malnourished. And if that doesn't work, we can always build more prisons.

One of the most troubling consequences of the bias against non-pharmaceutical approaches to disease has been the failure of all forms of cancer research to make serious inroads into cancer mortality in the industrialized world. The two great successes in the struggle against cancer – the reductions in deaths caused by lung and stomach cancer – have taken place entirely independently of the research into treatments conducted by the corporations, the major cancer charities, the universities and state institutions. The discovery that bacterial infections cause gastric ulcers may have inadvertently saved more people from stomach cancer than all the research done to date by those seeking a cure for it.[39] And just as the major corporations and the cancer research charities have had very little to do with the declines in some forms of cancer, they have little to say about the increases in other kinds. The commercial value of new cancer drugs should not distract independent researchers from seeking ways to prevent the disease through changes in lifestyle and improvements to the environment. Yet the major cancer charities show an overwhelming bias towards diagnosis and treatment as opposed to prevention in their research. A quick review of the current research programmes of Britain's largest cancer research charity, Cancer Research UK, indicates that of 235 ongoing clinical trials, eighteen were classified under either 'prevention' or 'risks and causes'. Most of these eighteen trials looked at genetic factors in cancer risk. Fewer than 3 per cent of Cancer Research UK's trials at the time of writing looked at the role that environmental and dietary factors might play in causing or preventing cancer.[40]

Recent reports that suggest vitamin D deficiency might play a role in the development of certain cancers have not been received enthusiastically by Cancer Research UK. An epidemiologist from the charity, Laura Yochum, pointed out that many studies have failed to establish a link. But it could be argued that a cancer research charity ought to spend more of its time exploring how improvements in diet and environment might reduce the incidence of cancer, and less time doing the kind of work that could be left to commercial operations. By adopting an almost identical research agenda to that of the pharmaceutical corporations, medical charities might be missing an important opportunity to reduce the suffering and premature death caused by preventable but incurable forms of the disease.[41] If they are going to spend almost no time or money researching environmental and dietary factors in cancer risk, they ought at least to make that clear to their donors and the general public.

To return to the SSRIs, the comparative research done to date seems to show that a combination of drug and cognitive behavioural therapy offers the best outcome for those suffering from moderate to severe depression. Not only that, combined therapies do not require prolonged use of the drug. A course of treatment is exactly that; it is not a euphemism for long-term and even lifelong use. Even though the National Institute for Clinical Excellence in the UK has recommended combining cognitive behavioural therapy (CBT) and drug therapy for moderate to severe depression since

December 2004, in Britain combined therapy is still offered to fewer than half of those for whom it is the most appropriate form of treatment.[42] CBT was invented in the 1960s, more than twenty years before the SSRIs were hailed as a miracle cure for depression.

Incidentally, the heavy marketing of Prozac and the other SSRIs has created a great deal of confusion in the general public. Many of us now believe that 'serotonin levels fall when we feel low, and this lowering is thought to affect everything from our diets, to how we educate our children and how we manage criminality. But there is no evidence for any of this, nor has there ever been. A huge gap has opened up between what is scientifically demonstrable and what people believe, pointing to a cultural phenomenon that lies well beyond the "medicalization" so worrying to sociologists and bio-ethicists.'[43] This gap between public beliefs and the scientific basis for them bears comparison with the most outlandish clams of holistic and alternative therapists. Indeed the mythical accounts of mental illness promoted by the pharmaceutical system present a much more serious threat to the proper conduct of science. Rather than openly defying conventional science, the serotonin deficiency myth borrows from, and betrays, its prestige.

The safety or otherwise of pharmaceutical drugs and other industrial products has been the source of career-ending controversy for many scientists. Only a particularly naive researcher can now imagine that their findings will be welcome if they threaten powerful institutional interests. As universities and regulatory agencies move closer to business, scientists will come under increasing pressure to accommodate their new 'partners'; concerns about public health cannot automatically win out over commercial considerations. In such circumstances prudent scientists must be tempted to avoid looking at aspects of reality where powerful institutions have a vested interest. Seeing colleagues who stand by inconvenient findings suddenly lose status, reputation and even livelihood serves to warn other scientists that objective truth is all very well most of the time, but shouldn't be allowed to ruin a promising career. A little bit of sophistication, a certain way with the data, and perhaps the results aren't quite so conclusive as they might seem to those determined to create obstacles to progress. This threat to individual scientists comes from within the scientific institutions themselves, and is much more likely to destroy the innocent curiosity of the researcher than any real or imagined tide of unreason outside.[44]

Most of us depend on hierarchical institutions for status and even material sustenance. Under the circumstances it is unreasonable to imagine that scientists and technicians will recklessly risk their positions and their peace of mind by making public statements in a context that offers no real hope of bringing change. David Graham's appearance in the Senate offered him a rare chance to appeal directly to those who had the power to reform the FDA. In these circumstances, silence about widespread failings in the regulatory system became, for him, morally untenable. Most scientists never have such a chance and can hardly be blamed for remaining silent. Even when an opportunity does arrive, the experiences of Graham and others must act as a powerful deterrent against excessive candour. We must assume that the threat to science posed by corporations and states is greatly under-reported.

In such circumstances polemics against 'alternative' medicine aren't as daringly enlightened as they seem at first glance. The follies of faith healers, *reiki* specialists and reflexologists provide good knockabout copy, and sometimes the fringe practitioners do cause harm when they stop patients from seeking effective treatment as promptly as they might. But the public's appetite for alternatives to 'orthodox medicine' does not simply derive from a foolish disregard for scientific reason. The public has started to notice that there are serious problems in the structure and conduct of conventional medicine. An enlightened defence of clinical science would seek to restore the public's faith in doctors by recognizing and seeking to address these problems. This must mean reforming the relationship between science and the pharmaceutical industry in ways that are bound to displease the corporations. As Adriane Fugh-Berman, an associate professor at Georgetown University School of Medicine, points out, 'The drug industry is happy to play the generous and genial uncle until physicians want to discuss subjects that are off limits, such as the benefits of diet or exercise, or the relationship between medicine and pharmaceutical companies.'[45] When Taverne and others focus on the excesses of alternative medicine without registering the sometimes much more lethal failings of orthodox medicine, they mislead even as they, doubtless sincerely, seek to enlighten.

Think tanks and intellectuals, often funded by corporations, insist on the need to defend science from its enemies. Groups like Sense about Science in the UK and the American Council on Science and Health (ACSH) focus almost exclusively on the irrational enemies of science – they set out to champion a scientific, evidence-based approach in areas of controversy; yet they largely overlook any evidence that corporations themselves might, where commercially threatened, pose a threat to free inquiry. The website of the ACSH proclaims that it 'was founded in 1978 by a group of scientists who had become concerned that many important public policies related to health and the environment did not have a sound scientific basis'.[46] Since then it has reliably defended industry from criticism and 'has stood as a bulwark against the contemporary Luddites who see the beginning of civilization's end in every technological advance that reaches the market place'.[47] To take one example, its medical director, Gilbert Ross, has written of the Vioxx disaster that 'the case can be made that both Merck and the FDA acted responsibly throughout this episode. Early on, the trials and initial post-marketing studies did not show significant data of increased risk from Vioxx.'[48] As we have seen, this directly contradicts expert testimony from Gurkirpal Singh, David Graham and others.

The attempt to establish corporations as the champions of science and their opponents as irrational scaremongers has had some success among those in the scientific establishment. Set up by the Royal Institution to tackle an 'emerging anti-science mood', the Science Media Centre (SMC) in London drew on a panel of experts to establish its founding principles. Although one of the experts consulted suggested that the SMC might 'provide access to dissident voices on science from NGOs and protest groups', and perhaps invite them on to the board of governors, the majority 'had a slightly different starting point'. The SMC's board of governors has no representatives from any NGO or protest group, but it does include an employee of Luther Pendragon, a strategic communications consultancy whose clients include Syngenta, a Swiss pesticides manufacturer, and the American restaurant chain McDonald's.[49]

In 2005 the outgoing head of the UK's Royal Society, Lord May, warned at length about the threat to the Enlightenment posed by fundamentalist religion while noting only in passing the climate-change denial lobby. Despite the fact that Lord May is deeply concerned about the impact of climate change, and indeed compares it with weapons of mass destruction as a threat to human life, it is the 'resurgent fundamentalism, East and West' that threatens the enlightened inheritance. Lord May's concern about irrational threats to science makes sense as long as corporate claims to be pro-science are taken at face value.[50]

The enlightened defence of science as elaborated by the likes of Furedi and Taverne, and as accepted by much of the scientific establishment, has an inescapably paradoxical nature. The corporate threat to free inquiry is downplayed or obscured entirely and the always ambiguous and often downright fraudulent claims of corporations to be pro-science are endorsed by the self-styled champions of Enlightenment. Meanwhile even though we distrust science because it is unduly influenced by special interests, our distrust is taken as evidence that more must be done to resist the 'march of unreason' and to 'restore public faith in science'. That is to say, more must be done to reconcile us to the current system of corporate domination. Those who oppose corporate power become part of an 'irrational' reaction against science and progress. As with hostility to Evangelical religion, campaigns against holistic and alternative approaches to human health leave unexamined the much more pressing threats to reason posed by entirely rational agents operating within the institutions responsible for much of the conduct of science.

Of course, we should resist attempts by fundamentalists to distort science. And when scientists face intimidation and physical danger from anti-abortionists or anti-vivisectionists, they must have protection from the state and the support of the public. But we should also recognize the scale and the seriousness of the threat posed to science by institutions that situate themselves within the Enlightenment tradition. If we chunter on about mumbo-jumbo and the march of unreason, we prevent ourselves and a wider public from grasping the facts of the matter. By offering us a chance to feel resentful and anxious about the alleged power of unreason, the Folk Enlightenment obscures the forces that menace individual scientists, distort the research agenda and threaten to destroy science as a humane endeavour.[51]

6

Postmodernism and the Assault on Truth

Enlightenment behaves towards things as a dictator towards men.
Theodor W. Adorno and Max Horkheimer,
Dialectic of Enlightenment (1947)

There is another threat to reason that features regularly in the
writings of the Folk Enlightenment: postmodernism, which is
supposed to menace all that we value about the enlightened
inheritance. As a style in thought, its influence has been pervasive
in intellectual culture, according to two energetic defenders of the
Enlightenment, the writers Ophelia Benson and Jeremy Stan-
groom:

> Many books and articles have appeared, raising an eyebrow and
> smiling an incredulous smile at concepts such as rationality, well-
> conducted enquiry, evidence, inference, warrant, justification,
> the Enlightenment project, universalism, science and truth.[1]

Frank Furedi claims that this scepticism about the truth has had a
widespread and disastrous effect on public life in Britain:

> It is frequently argued that there is no such thing as truth. Instead
> of the truth, people are exhorted to accept different opinions as
> representing many truths. Michel Foucault's claim that there is
> no 'truly universal truth' has gained widespread acceptance in
> academic circles. Truth is rarely represented as an objective fact; it

is frequently portrayed as the product of subjective insight, which is in competition with other equally valid perspectives. Relativism – a perspective that contends that conceptions of truth and moral values are not absolute but are relative to the persons or groups holding them – has acquired a commanding influence over cultural life.[2]

But what exactly is this thing, postmodernism, that threatens modern, enlightened, civilization? Trying to define it is not easy since, as Furedi remarks, 'postmodernists tend to eschew definitions',[3] but most of us will be familiar with the description provided by its opponents: postmodernism caricatures science, mocks the idea of progress and challenges the very idea that it might be possible to discover the truth. Postmodernists claim that something called the Enlightenment Project led Western civilization directly to the Gulag and the Final Solution:

> In the standard postmodernist demonology, the Enlightenment bears direct historical responsibility for the Gulag and Auschwitz. In the eyes of these convinced misologists, modern totalitarianism is merely the upshot of the universalizing impetus of the Enlightenment. As Foucault proclaimed, 'Raison, c'est la torture.'[4]

According to their critics, postmodernists set themselves against what they call 'the tyranny of reason' and advocate radical scepticism about the possibility of objective truth and moral certainty. They object to mathematics on the grounds that it is gendered, and they spend their time writing articles with titles like 'Transgressing the boundaries: Towards a transformative hermeneutics of quantum gravity'.[5] So Alan Sokal and Jean Bricmont describe postmodernism as 'an intellectual current characterised by the more-or-less explicit rejection of the rationalist tradition of the Enlightenment, by theoretical discourses disconnected from any empirical test, and by a cognitive and cultural relativism that regards science as nothing more than a "narration", a myth, or a social construction among many others'.[6]

'Postmodernism', a maddeningly imprecise word, can perhaps be understood more clearly in historical terms, as a response to the accumulated disasters of Western modernity from the nineteenth century through to the 1960s: imperialism, world war and genocide. Postmodernism responds to the ways in which powerful institutions and individuals used ideas of modernity to justify, and modern technology to execute, unspeakable crimes. Imperialists brought Enlightenment to the peoples they conquered.[7] So President McKinley was praised after his death for bringing the Philippines 'out of the thraldom and darkness of three hundred years into the liberty and enlightenment of the twentieth century'.[8] The enthusiastic nationalism of intellectual elites throughout Europe in the First World War was described in terms of *kultur* and civilization. Stalinists insisted that their brutal policies were justified by the need to defend the workers' state, and with it the chance of total liberation for all mankind. Even the Nazis added a delight in technology and pseudo-Darwinism to their brand of vacuous and energetic irrationalism. Scientific rationality itself became suspect under the conditions of global war. Technical experts enthusiastically lent their skills and ingenuity to the various obscenities of modern weaponry, from Fritz Haber's poison gas and the triumph of the physicists in the skies over Hiroshima, to the defoliants and napalm of the 1960s. In literature and fine art, notions of absolute value and objective standards of merit came under suspicion as the extent of the US state's Cold War manipulations became clear. The CIA played an important covert role in subsidizing and promoting high modernism as a riposte to socialist realism. Enlightenment had been repeatedly used as an alibi or plea in mitigation by the dominant forces in the world. Faced with this confident and criminal modernity, some writers associated with postmodernism came to define themselves in terms of their 'incredulity towards metanarratives';[9] the idea of progress that had animated Europe since the seventeenth century became an object of radical scepticism.

The origins of postmodernism are very varied, but one of the most important works to call the idea of Enlightenment into question is Theodor W. Adorno and Max Horkheimer's *Dialectic of Enlightenment*. First published in 1947, the book is an anguished response above all to the horrors of the Second World War. In it, the authors argue that Francis Bacon's ambitions for science as a means of mastering nature have encoded a programme of domination into the Enlightenment's language of progress and liberation. Implicit in Bacon's scientific and philosophical work is a lively appreciation of the material advantages that the scientific method would bring to the powers that commanded it. In 'In praise of human knowledge' (1592), Bacon writes:

> But indeed facility to believe, impatience to doubt, temerity to answer, glory to know, doubt to contradict, end to gain, sloth to search, seeking things in words, resting in part of nature; these and the like have been the things which have forbidden the happy match between the mind of man and the nature of things; and in place thereof have married it to vain notions and blind experiments: and what the posterity and issue of so honourable a match may be, it is not hard to consider. Printing, a gross invention; artillery, a thing that lay not far out of the way; the needle, a thing partly known before: what a change have these three things made in the world in these times; the one in the state of learning, the other in the state of war, the third in the state of treasure, commodities and navigation! And those, I say, were but stumbled upon and lighted upon by chance. Therefore, no doubt, the sovereignty of man lieth hid in knowledge; wherein many things are reserved, which kings with their treasure cannot buy, nor by their force command; their spials and intelligencers can give no news of them, their seamen and discoverers cannot sail where they grow: now we govern nature in opinions, but we are in thrall to her in necessity: but if we would be led by her in invention, we should command her by action.[10]

Here then, according to its critics, is the original sin of Enlightenment. The inquiry into the world by the experimental method was for Bacon explicitly a campaign of conquest. Adorno and Horkheimer claim that 'what men want to learn from nature is how to use it in order wholly to dominate it and other men'. The world of nature is disenchanted and becomes an object of knowledge. This knowledge of the world has no limits; 'Knowledge, which is power, knows no obstacles . . .'[11] Eventually the disenchantment of nature extends to our fellow human beings and in this way Enlightenment transforms us into objects of rational administration. Hence the formulation that has quickened the blood of undergraduates for more than half a century, 'Enlightenment is totalitarian'[12] – its insatiable appetite for control over nature relates closely, albeit in ways that are not fully explained, to political tyranny: 'Enlightenment behaves towards things as a dictator towards men. He knows them insofar as he can manipulate them.'

Adorno and Horkheimer were acutely aware that Bacon's new science had a disruptive impact that he himself had not predicted. They always intended their book 'to prepare the way for a positive notion of enlightenment which will release it from entanglement in blind domination.'[13] Unlike some of their more excitable readers, they remained deeply ambivalent about the meaning and future of Enlightenment. On the one hand they were aware that Enlightenment contained a potentially ungovernable challenge to established power: 'And knowledge, in which Bacon was certain "the sovereignty of man lay hid", can now become the dissolution of domination.' On the other, they saw that powerful forces were set on preventing this: 'But in the face of such a possibility, and in the service of the present age, enlightenment becomes the wholesale deception of the masses'.[14] In the end, as Stephen Bronner argues, the attempt made in *Dialect of Enlightenment* to prepare the way for a positive notion of Enlightenment fails, since the authors cannot finally establish how Enlightenment could ever free itself from its origins in Bacon's imperial ambitions for knowledge.

Those influenced by Adorno and Horkheimer came to believe that no political response was possible to a regime of rational and enlightened domination – a totally administered society. Instead they sought to avoid personal incorporation into an industrialized cultural order through the 'aesthetic–philosophical intensification of subjectivity'.[15] Those who believe that 'Enlightenment is totalitarian' seek consolation in a 'private' life of detailed and energetic discrimination. Adorno's Californian exile, with its air-conditioning, classical music and homesickness, provides a romanticized model for this disastrous retreat into the 'aesthetic' sphere. The rigorous distinction between a 'private' life of culture and refinement and a 'public' life of compromises conducted in an ironic style disguises the extent to which such a form of life embodies total subordination to the logic of corporate production. In such cases, common in modern business, the exercise of independent intelligence provides a restorative holiday from 'the real world' of work. It does not engage critically with it. The discerning, civilized self survives as a strictly recreational identity. The old ideal of intellectual and artistic autonomy degenerates into a lifestyle, a set of choices about one's leisure activities, a form of 'power-protected inwardness'.[16]

We can certainly trace one history of Enlightenment from Bacon to the British Empire and on to the modern global administration. The insurgent European powers of the period after 1700 depended heavily on the 'enlightened' institutions for a technological base that in turn powered global domination. The desire for total knowledge, in the service of total power, that we find in the Department of Defense and the Ministry of Defence is an expression of Enlightenment. But this history must ignore the sense of Enlightenment as freedom of inquiry and freedom to publish. For the Enlightenment could not be contained within those institutions and their equivalents in Soviet Russia and Nazi Germany. Enlightenment informed the movements of national and social liberation within and outside Europe as surely as it informed the colonial powers' war-making technology. The military-industrial Enlightenment, the Occult Enlightenment, is certainly the world's governing contradiction in terms. It is a machine for absorbing information and radiating deception. Within it, the history of Enlightenment, its methods, even the enlightened attitude towards knowledge, serve the purposes of domination. Enlightenment is lavished with hypocritical

praise by the powerful because the enlightened have proved so carelessly productive of new opportunities for profit and new methods of coercion. But Enlightenment does not belong to the powerful and their experts entirely. The guileless desire to discover and share the truth bears within it a finally ungovernable capacity to escape its institutional bonds and put itself at the service of liberation.

Still, the postmodern concern that Enlightenment and modernity can provide cover for crimes has ample justification. Enlightened ideals have often proved valuable to those who seek power by deception and violence. Opponents can be denounced for being 'unenlightened' in a move that is often highly persuasive to those who consider themselves forward-looking and rational. So during the debate about NAFTA, the North American Free Trade Association, the liberal commentator Anthony Lewis wrote in a tone of sorrowful disappointment that:

> The arguments made against NAFTA by such significant opponents as the United Auto Workers seem to me to come down to fear of change and fear of foreigners . . . Unions in this country, sad to say, are looking more and more like the British unions that have become such a millstone around the neck of the Labor Party: backward, unenlightened . . .[17]

Commentators in the mainstream media largely agreed. NAFTA was a 'free-trade agreement' and free trade was a good thing, so resistance to it could only be irrational. In fact, fears that the agreement would damage the livelihoods of the poor in both the United States and Mexico have proved well-founded. According to Sandra Polaski of the Carnegie Endowment for International Peace, since 1994 'the jobs created in the manufacturing industry have not kept pace with jobs lost in the agricultural sector' in Mexico; furthermore, NAFTA is responsible for 'a surge in migration' to the United States by the rural poor who 'have borne the brunt of adjustment to NAFTA'.[18]

Those who threaten state interests are repeatedly accused of

being 'unenlightened'. If they are very unlucky they can be 'enlightened' by force, as in the Philippines in the late nineteenth century, and in a series of missionary expeditions since then. Soldiers have sometimes seen through the pious language that accompanies their foreign adventures. Speaking in 1931, the former US Marines' Major General Smedley Butler explained how he spent thirty-three years being 'a high-class muscle man for Big Business, Wall Street and the bankers': 'I helped purify Nicaragua for the international banking house of Brown Brothers in 1909–1912. I helped make Mexico and especially Tampico safe for American oil interest in 1916. I brought light to the Dominican Republic for American sugar interests in 1916.'[19] When SAS troopers kill people, they talk, with deep black humour, about 'giving them the good news'.

Like faith, Enlightenment can all too easily degenerate into a swindle. The prestige of revolutionary communism depended on its successful appropriation of the enlightened ideal of progress. Although the 'scientific' laws of dialectical materialism have gone the way of theosophy and the Mithras cult, they appeared to the socialists of the late nineteenth century as, at last, a scientific description of the social world – as a 'truly universal truth' that granted believers insight into both the history and the future of the human race. And so what if the inexorable logic of history calls for bloodshed? Carnage in the service of perfect freedom is not a crime. Or so it seemed to many entirely sincere communists.

To a degree that is deeply unsettling for anyone who wants to maintain a strict distinction between liberal and totalitarian regimes, British liberal imperialism in the nineteenth century drew comfort from the idea of inevitable progress as it went about the melancholy work of extermination in Africa and Asia. A republican and a progressive at home, the Liberal politician Charles Dilke wrote in 1867, after a tour of the United States and the British colonies, that 'The Anglo-Saxon is the only extirpating race on earth. Up to the commencement of the now inevitable destruction of the Red Indians of Central North America, of the Maories, and of the Australians by the English colonists, no numerous race had ever

been blotted out by an invader.'[20] There is no doubt that for Dilke this was a good, even a great thing:

> Everywhere we have found that the difficulties that impede the progress to universal domination of the English people lie in the conflict with the cheaper races. The result of our survey is such as to give good reason for the belief that race distinctions will long continue, that miscegenation will go but a little way towards blending races; that the dearer are, on the whole, likely to destroy the cheaper peoples, and that Saxondom will rise triumphant from the doubtful struggle.[21]

Remarking on the difference between American and British attitudes towards 'extirpation', he pointed out that:

> There is in these matters less hypocrisy among the Americans than with ourselves. In 1840, the British Government assumed the sovereignty of New Zealand in a proclamation which set forth with great precision that it did so for the sole purpose of protecting the aborigines in the possession of their lands. The Maories numbered 200,000 then; they number 20,000 now.[22]

The 'Indian Question' in America was to be resolved, Dilke observed, by a programme of extermination: 'rifle and revolver are their only policy'.[23]

Many intellectuals considered eugenics a necessary, if in some senses unfortunate, step towards a world without misery and poverty: 'It is better for all the world, if instead of waiting to execute degenerate offspring for crime, or to let them starve for their imbecility, society can prevent those who are manifestly unfit from continuing their kind,' declared Supreme Court Justice Oliver Wendell Holmes in 1926.[24] John Maynard Keynes, George Bernard Shaw and many other progressives supported eugenics, at least for a time. Postmodern caution about the claims of intellectuals to be guided by such 'scientific' principles is at its best a wholly justifiable response to this history.

Postmodernism's popularity in the American academy from the 1960s onwards in part derived from the close involvement of liberal scholars and experts in an increasingly demented Cold War against the Soviet Union and her real and imaginary allies. The New Deal coalition of labour unions, liberal academics and the Democrat Party had been maintained and expanded during the Second World War and formed the basis for America's political directorate in the early years of the Cold War. This collaboration between a liberal and progressive state and idealistic intellectuals in the Kennedy White House resulted in the pacification and democratization campaigns in Vietnam and in the security assistance programme provided to governments in Central and South America. This so-called 'Alliance for Progress' became, through the alchemy of the national security state, the means by which Latin American armies were transformed into paramilitary organizations that could be used against internal enemies. Under the aegis of John F. Kennedy and Lyndon B. Johnson, liberal intellectuals enthusiastically sought to defeat racism and poverty at home and communism abroad. Yet, as it became clear to increasing numbers of Americans that the war in Vietnam was indefensible, the complicity of liberal intellectuals such as Robert McNamara in that country's destruction did much to demoralize the remaining supporters of the New Deal. The enlightened spirit of public engagement that had mobilized academia to combat the Depression a generation earlier had by the mid-sixties degenerated into auxiliary support for a spectacularly lethal war against a people trying to govern their own affairs.

Faced with the facts of this collaboration, academics sought to restore some sense of moral integrity to the work they did. The radical scepticism about objective truth they found in Continental philosophy seemed to be some kind of answer. In the social sciences, for example, anthropologists 'began a systematic interrogation of the contemporary state of the discipline as well as of the colonial circumstances from which it had emerged and the same impulse led to similar moves in other disciplines.'[25] After Vietnam and the Alliance for Progress in South America, academics no longer believed that enlightened intellectuals working within a liberal state could provide an adequate basis for a renewed Enlightenment. In this sense, the postmodern turn in America is perhaps better understood as an attempt to put knowledge beyond the use of state power, rather than as some kind of assault on reason. For while we can agree with Bronner that 'no historical or political justification exists for claiming that Anglo-American liberalism turned into its totalitarian opposite',[26] even the avowedly and sincerely democratic and peaceful experts of the 1960s cannot avoid responsibility for the obscenity of 'democratization' and 'pacification'. Nostalgia for the New Deal should not blind us to the historical crimes of the liberal and democratic state. These crimes are less obvious to us than those of Hitler and Stalin. Still-existing power works hard to diminish or obscure them. But they are still crimes, crimes on a vast scale, and we cannot remain honest and ignore them.

The enlightened world of science and technical expertise continues to entangle itself in the world of blind domination. Social scientists still seek the prestige and material rewards that come from making themselves useful to states and corporations. For example, 'strategic demography' uses statistical analysis of populations to help construct social and foreign policy.[27] The most influential product of this discipline is the so-called 'Youth Bulge' theory:

> Developed in 1985 by geographer Gary Fuller during a stint as visiting scholar in the Central Intelligence Agency's (CIA's) Office of Global Issues, formal 'youth bulge' theory originally aimed to provide US intelligence analysts with a tool to predict unrest and uncover potential national security threats. It claims that a proportion of more than 20 per cent of young people in a population signals the possibility of political rebellion and unrest. It equates large percentages of young men with an increased possibility of violence, particularly in the South, where, analysts argue, governments may not have the capacity to support them.[28]

This notion, with its air of scientific respectability and powerful institutional support, has provided a helpful explanation for Middle

Eastern hostility to the United States. But while based on accurate data it goes far beyond that data to provide a kind of weaponized understanding of the world. Demography becomes destiny and science lends its authority to myth. For example, in an October 2001 report in *Newsweek* entitled 'Why do they hate us?' part of the answer ran as follows: 'Arab societies are going through a massive youth bulge, with more than half of most countries' populations under the age of 25 . . . A huge influx of restless young men in any country is bad news. When accompanied by even small economic and social change, it usually produces a new politics of protest.'[29]

A similar mythopoeia surrounds many notions in mainstream social science, such as the 'underclass' and the 'resource war'. As in the case of 'youth bulge' theory, the 'resource war' strips human agency from events and replaces them with some overriding, external cause, whether it be drought, declining oil reserves or a youth bulge. The fact that a resource is scarce magically explains and justifies armed conflict and is used to obscure the ways in which conflict might be averted through political compromise or technological change. In a period of deepening environmental crisis, myths prepare us for a future of proliferating violence by deploying facts from the sciences in illegitimate ways. So, for example, two Pentagon analysts decide that abrupt changes in global temperatures will usher in a new epoch of violent conflict; 'disruption and conflict will be endemic features of life.'[30] In a similar way, overlapping misapprehensions, confusions and misinformation from the social sciences together contribute to the grand myths that sustain both the 'War on Drugs' and the related category 'Organized Crime'.

Any attempt to revive the Enlightenment must address the challenge of postmodernism honestly. In some respects this challenge is important and historically justified. Scientific research can give a spurious kind of cover to repressive policies. Powerful institutions exert considerable overt and covert influence over the objectives of research. The prestige of science can be used to suppress dissent. The doctrine of progress and the authority of science have provided justifications for some of the worst atrocities in human history. These justifications were specious, but they were believed sincerely by people who considered themselves enlightened. We cannot allow ourselves to be complacent about what constitutes science or supine before any statement that claims to be rational or reasonable. This is not to say that postmodernism has had a wholly benign influence. Some of its representative figures do conform to the stereotype beloved of their enemies, of crude relativism and obscurantism. But even at its most excessive and wrong-headed, postmodernism hardly registers as a threat to reason when compared with the forces that intertwine with both social and physical science and seek to render knowledge safe for state and private institutions.

I don't think that we can or should accept the identification of Enlightenment with totalitarianism that some postmodernists have taken from *Dialectic of Enlightenment*. Reason and science can be employed for swindling ends, but they can also serve in the cause of human liberation. The decision to treat human beings as objects of rational administration does not derive from the operations of rationality. It is an act of will. Rather than abandoning Enlightenment to the occult practitioners of total science – a science conducted without humane restraint – we must understand more clearly the conflict, always implicit in the Enlightenment, between political and economic power, and the hope of a world remade. It is to this conflict that we now turn.

7

An Actually Existing Infamy

Ecrasez l'infâme.
Kill the Monster.
Voltaire

I have so far tried to show that the Folk Enlightenment is both ubiquitous and mistaken; it provides a structure for understanding many issues of pressing importance, from the War on Terror to debates about the role of science in society. But it cannot justify its pre-eminent position in contemporary debate on any factual basis. The most serious threats to reason in Britain and America do not come from the commonly cited enemies of the Enlightenment, those unlikely coalitions of the Old Testament and the New Age. Our concerns should be proportionate to the threats we face, if we are to be justified in considering ourselves enlightened. It follows that we should concentrate on the most significant threats to reason. For this is where the serious work is to be done, even if it means risking disorientation, confusion and error.

The state and the corporation, the institutions that between them provide the setting for the Occult Enlightenment, clearly pose a very serious threat to public understanding. Even those who benefit from the patronage of both these classes of institution and identify closely with them have, I think, been shocked in recent years by the deceptions of both the state and the corporate sector. The accounting scandals that engulfed Enron, World.com, Andersen and many other companies in 2001 and 2002, combined with the US-UK propaganda campaign for the invasion of Iraq in 2003, have contributed to a greatly increased awareness of the impact that false or misleading information from official sources can have on public attempts at rational decision-making. Yet it is important that we recognize that these ham-fistedly obvious attempts to distort or suppress the truth have their origins in a much wider and deeper system of mendacity and violence.

The US and UK states have a bewildering range of functions, from welfare to warfare. The states contradict themselves, they contain multitudes.[1] But these states are not only bewildering because of their great complexity. They are made more mysterious by the fact that many of their activities are shrouded in secrecy. Our ability to understand the world, and hence our ability to make informed political decisions, must certainly be affected by the culture of secrecy that surrounds the operations of government. This secrecy intensifies around the security, intelligence and defence institutions. On 10 September 2001, Donald Rumsfeld, the then US Secretary of Defense, told a Pentagon audience that 'according to some estimates, we cannot track $2.3 trillion in transactions'.[2] By way of comparison, total federal expenditure is around $2.2 trillion annually. Rumsfeld didn't explain how long it took to lose sight of the $2.3 trillion, and indeed gave no further details; the figure was mentioned in passing, almost casually. A later report revealed that the Pentagon's auditors still couldn't account adequately for 25 per cent of the money it spent.[3] In such circumstances it is hard to see in what sense we are living in cultures that can claim, in Paul Berman's phrase, 'to inculcate public habits of rational decision-making'.[4] Indeed this absence of accountability makes it difficult to imagine that we live under anything approaching openly enlightened conditions.

State secrecy has always been as much a matter of protecting the internal character and workings of the state from public scrutiny as it has been about denying information to the enemy. The notion that a free media and democratic institutions make secrecy impossible is itself profoundly deceptive. Writing in his memoirs, the former Department of Defense employee Daniel Ellsberg notes that:

It is a commonplace that 'you can't keep secrets in Washington' or 'in a democracy', that 'no matter how sensitive the secret, you're likely to read it the next day in the *New York Times*'. These truisms are flatly false. They are in fact cover stories, ways of flattering and misleading journalists and their readers, part of the process of keeping secrets well . . . [T]he fact is that the over-whelming majority of secrets do not leak to the American public. This is true even when the information withheld is well known to an enemy and when it is clearly essential to the functioning of the congressional war power and to any democratic control of foreign policy. The reality unknown to the public and to most members of Congress and the press is that secrets that would be of the greatest import to many of them can be kept from them reliably for decades by the executive branch, even though they are known to thousands of insiders.[5]

Ellsberg gives an example of this. In the course of defending the official account of events in the Gulf of Tonkin Incident, the pretext for America's escalating involvement in the Vietnam War, US officials and responsible journalists used to point out that any deception would have required the active collusion of thousands of people. Yet the American people *were* deceived about exactly what happened in the Gulf of Tonkin and thousands of people *did* know it. US presidents from Kennedy to Nixon were able to execute a secret foreign policy during the war in Vietnam. It would be naive in the extreme to imagine that it is more difficult now.[6]

Official secrecy, the level of knowledge shared by hundreds, even thousands, of government employees, can itself act as an admin-istrative resource, even as yet another instrument of deception. The American Edmond Taylor moved from journalism to working first at the Office of Strategic Services (OSS) and later at the Psycho-logical Strategy Board (PSB). Writing of his work there, he explained how:

I gradually came to realise . . . [that] the feeling that one had at last got behind the scenes of history was to a large extent an illusory one. The staff of PSB ranked fairly highly in the Washington hierarchy of documentary security clearance, but, I soon discovered, above the nominal aristocracy of Top Secret, Cosmic or Q-Clearance holders there was an inner super-elite contemptuous of all classificatory ritualism, whose thoughts were so arcane that they were seldom committed to paper at all, at least not in any official form. As one of these Great Initiates revealed to me in a rare moment of confidence . . . the US, like many other nations, has two levels of national policy, the exoteric and the esoteric. The former found its expression in the papers of the NSC [National Security Council] . . . As to the esoteric policy my informant's lips were naturally sealed.[7]

Beneath the NSC's supposedly 'fundamental conflict' between the idea of slavery and the idea of freedom during the Cold War lay the American state's 'esoteric' policies. Much of this 'esoteric' national policy can be guessed at with a fair degree of confidence by anyone willing to look at that country's foreign policy since 1945. But an accurate description of the state's real character will be associated with a large and noisy lunatic fringe; it will be consigned to the peripheries of debate, alongside those who believe that aliens or witches control the world. A sensible caution about official secrecy will be dismissed by many academic historians, for whom top secret documents are the final authority in establishing policy goals. But the fact that, as a well-connected insider, Taylor felt excluded from the inner circle of decision-making suggests that the state's capacity to disguise its true nature and intentions from its own technical experts is essentially unlimited. Through its system of rewards and punishments, it largely retains its 'esoteric' character. To put it another way, in order to be taken seriously as an expert on the state one must be able to ignore the very real possibility that its nature and purposes are at odds with the official record.

Examples abound of the way in which states combine secrecy about their institutional natures with manipulative programmes to persuade the public to support particular objectives. In a speech in 1993 relating his experiences in Washington as a journalist at

Associated Press and *Newsweek*, Robert Parry explained how the US government ignored US law and used the CIA's expertise in psychological warfare to secure domestic support for a terrorist campaign against the leftist government in Nicaragua in the early 1980s. This wasn't a matter of countering foreign disinformation and providing information to assist rational decision-making. This was about pressing buttons: 'The documentation is . . . clear that the idea was to find our "hot buttons" and to see what – how they could turn, twist, spin certain information to appeal to various special groups. They'd reached the point, and this was really being directed by the CIA, of breaking down the American people into subgroups.' Themes were developed to appeal to particular sub-groups. Journalists were likely to be concerned about the freedom of the press, so they were targeted with stories about Sandinista harassment of *La Prensa*, a Nicaraguan newspaper opposed to the government; Jewish Americans were told that the Sandinistas were anti-Semitic. Eventually, the CIA's 'perception managers' came up with something that played on popular xenophobia and worked particularly well in states on the border with Mexico:

> [They'd] found out that most of the themes about the commu-
> nist menace in Central America left people cold. They didn't
> really take it that seriously – it just didn't hit the hot buttons right.
> But they found that one hot button that really . . . they could
> really use was this idea of the Hispanic immigrants flooding into
> the United States. So they developed what they called the 'feet
> people' argument, which was that unless we stopped the com-
> munists in Nicaragua and San Salvador, 10 per cent – they came
> up with that figure somewhere – 10 per cent of all the people in
> Central America and Mexico will flood the United States.[8]

In the run-up to the 2003 invasion of Iraq, themes were developed for particular audiences in a manner strikingly reminiscent of the perception management campaign that secured public support for Reagan's policies in Central America. Human rights abuses, Saddam Hussein's alleged assassination attempt on the President's father, links between Iraq and al Qaeda, fundamentalist fears that 'Babylon' stalked the 'Holy Land', all found their way into the mix. The emphasis increasingly fell on weapons of mass destruction, 'the one issue everyone could agree on'.[9] In a formula hardly conducive to rational decision-making by the American public, the then National Security Advisor Condoleezza Rice insisted that they couldn't delay invasion until they had proof that Saddam Hussein had nuclear weapons: 'We don't want the smoking gun to be a mushroom cloud'.[10] President Bush repeated the message: 'we cannot wait for the final proof – the smoking gun – that could come in the form of a mushroom cloud'.[11] The promotion of market-tested irrationality at the highest levels of the US administration calls to mind H. L. Mencken's cynical comment that 'the whole aim of practical politics is to keep the populace alarmed (and hence clamorous to be led to safety) by menacing it with an endless series of hobgoblins, all of them imaginary.'

In these circumstances, it is hardly surprising that the US military pays lively attention to the informational aspects of modern war-fighting. In the Pentagon's *Joint Vision 2020*, the notion of 'full spectrum dominance' is glossed as meaning that the US military can operate 'with access to and freedom to operate in all domains – space, sea, land, air, and information'.[12] The ambition is for control of information that has the potential to assist the enemy or hinder the freedom of action of the US military.

In the US state's discussions of full spectrum and information dominance, it is hard to find any meaningful distinction between peace and war or between military and civilian adversaries. Information dominance is to be maintained at all times and against all relevant threats. This is not to say that the American military concerns itself with trying to establish totalitarian thought control. They want only to control the overwhelming preponderance of information systems, including the mass and elite media, that have operational significance. As long as the military controls information that has implications for its freedom of action, the forms of a free press can be retained. Indeed, these forms themselves have potent propaganda value – are they not what we are fighting for, after all?

As two Pentagon planners, Jim Winters and John Griffin, helpfully point out, 'when dominance occurs, nothing done, makes any difference. We have sufficient knowledge to stop anything we don't want to occur, or do anything we want to do'.[13]

Since the invasion of Iraq in March 2003, the American military has killed thirteen journalists and two media assistants.[14] Casualties have included the senior British ITN journalist Terry Lloyd, and Reuters cameraman Taras Protsyuk, who died when an American tank opened fire on the Hotel Palestine in Baghdad. It has also managed to bomb the offices of al-Jazeera in both Kabul and Baghdad. The Pentagon justified the Kabul missile strike by claiming that al-Qaeda was active in the al-Jazeera office. Televised interviews with Taliban officials counted as al-Qaeda activity, as far as the American military was concerned.[15] After a missile attack on al-Jazeera's Baghdad office in April 2003, which killed journalist Tarek Ayoub, a spokesman for US Central Command insisted that the station 'was not and never had been a target'.[16] And in a narrow sense this might be true: as outlined in information-dominance doctrine, the US military were not attacking al-Jazeera itself, but the disruption its reporting was causing to US policy. This might explain why al-Jazeera journalist Ahmed Mansour came under fire in Fallujah during the April 2004 American assault on the city[17] and why, a few days later, Bush suggested to Blair that they bomb the Dubai headquarters of al-Jazeera.[18] In light of the US military's comments about the need to establish information dominance, independent journalists in future conflicts will be wise to assume that, under certain circumstances, they will be treated as legitimate targets.

It isn't a point of great philosophical subtlety, but it is worth stating that truth and reason are threatened most directly and most effectively by those who intimidate or kill journalists and witnesses to awkward events. Once witnesses in the 'wrong' place have been killed, those privileged to be in the 'right' place (behind the US army's forward positions, say) find themselves inevitably turned into instruments of political warfare. In the absence of truthful information about all aspects of an event, the output of the surviving media, however scrupulously obtained, becomes part of a wider deceit. And the killing of journalists is only the most blatant way in which states undermine public understanding. In such circumstances, it is eccentric in the extreme to focus exclusively on the threat to reason posed by fundamentalists and postmodernists.

As part of its efforts to ensure that the public continues to misunderstand its nature and purposes, the US state continues to maintain very close links with the entertainment industry. The military and the intelligence agencies provide access to photogenic technology and locations worth millions to those film-makers who accept the need for advice on controversial aspects of their screen-plays. Since 9/11 the film industry has moved even closer to the state. Hollywood producers met with Karl Rove immediately after the attacks to discuss the themes that would be helpful in the context of the war on terrorism. After the meeting Sherry Lansing, the chairwoman of Paramount Pictures, told reporters that 'All of us have this incredible need, this incredible urge to do something'.[19] As it happens, 9/11 took place against a background of patriotic television programmes and films. Steven Spielberg's *Band of Brothers* was broadcast in September 2001 and *Pearl Harbor* had been released a few months before. The following year saw the release of *We Were Soldiers*, a patriotic Vietnam War film, and *Black Hawk Down*, set in Somalia. In September 2003, Showtime, like Paramount a sub-sidiary of Viacom, premiered *DC9/11: Time of Crisis*, a hagiogra-phical account of Bush's conduct in September 2001.

After the 9/11 attacks, a committee of the Institute of Creative Technologies, a virtual-reality warfare simulator and think tank funded by the Pentagon, was asked by the government to brain-storm possible terrorist threats and ways of dealing with them. Those attending included 'screenwriter Steven E. De Souza (*Die Hard, Die Hard 2*), director Joseph Zito (*Delta Force One, Missing in Action*), and wackier creative types like David Fincher, Spike Jonze, and Mary Lambert'.[20] At the opening of the ICT in 1999 the integration of the state with the entertainment industry had prompted the president of the Motion Pictures Association of America to declare that 'Hollywood is not the entertainment capital of the world. Washington, DC is the entertainment capital of the world!'[21] The relationship between the state and the film industry in the United States has a long and inglorious history. The CIA covertly financed and distributed film versions of George Orwell's *Animal Farm* and *1984*, having altered the endings in pursuit of their own propaganda objectives.

The American military also makes extensive use of games technology in its recruitment efforts. *Full Spectrum Warrior* began as a training simulator and was later released as a commercial product. Appropriately enough, the game's designers 'implemented a steadicam, to convey the sense of an embedded reporter'. The action takes place in a generic urban setting in the Middle East.[22] Another game developed by the US military, *America's Army*, uses the likenesses of serving soldiers to help players identify more closely with the action.[23] Ubisoft, a French company that helped develop *America's Army*, employs a team of 'Frag Dolls', young and attractive female gamers with names like Seppuku and Valkyrie. The company uses them to promote the consequence-free excitement of *America's Army* at gaming conventions.[24]

This militarization of popular culture goes a long way towards explaining why modern entertainment media so rarely manage to describe the political world in a faintly credible way. The decisive influences in the creation of state policy remain hidden from the public inside a black box called 'the national interest'. Around it swirl the distracting and seductive images of the film and television industry.

The US state has also taken a lively interest in literary culture. In 1961 the Chief of the CIA's Covert Action Staff explained that:

Books differ from all other propaganda media primarily because one book can significantly change the reader's attitude and action to an extent unmatched by the impact of any other single medium . . . this is of course not true of all books at all times and with all readers – but it is true significantly often enough to make books the most important weapons of strategic (long-term) propaganda.[25]

By 1967 the CIA had been involved in the publication of more than a thousand books. According to the source quoted above, the CIA could:

> Get books published or distributed abroad without revealing any US influence, by covertly subsidizing foreign publication or booksellers. Get books published that should not be 'contaminated' by any overt tie-in with the US government, especially if the position of the author is 'delicate'. Get books published for operational reasons, regardless of commercial viability. Initiate and subsidize indigenous national or international organizations for book publishing or distributing purposes. Stimulate the writing of politically significant books by unknown foreign authors – either by directly subsidizing the author, if covert contact is feasible, or indirectly, through literary agents or publishers.[26]

Books published with assistance from the CIA during the Cold War included a Swahili translation of Niccolò Machiavelli's *The Prince*, a Russian translation of T. S. Eliot's *The Waste Land*,[27] Kot Jelenski's *History and Hope: Progress in Freedom* and Boris Pasternak's *Dr Zhivago*.[28] The CIA's interest in the literary scene extended to book reviews. In a now notorious document the CIA set out a strategy for dealing with criticisms of the Warren Commission's report into the assassination of John Kennedy. As well as conversations with 'friendly elite contacts (especially politicians and editors)', agents were to 'employ propaganda assets . . . to refute the attacks of the critics. Book reviews and feature articles are particularly appropriate for this purpose.'[29]

The corporations also work hard both to disguise their nature and to influence public opinion. Though required by US law to subordinate all other considerations to the interests of their shareholders, they insist loudly on their essential benevolence and humanity. Yet, as the neoliberal economist Milton Friedman once remarked, all talk of 'corporate social responsibility' is like 'putting a good-looking woman in front of an automobile to sell an automobile'.[30] The sums spent on good-looking women and other tricks of the trade are very considerable. As well as in-house public relations, the corporations employ external consultants and make strategic contributions to charitable causes that help enhance their individual and collective image.

The public relations industry has always sought scientific means to prevent public resistance to its clients' actions. One of the founding fathers of modern propaganda, Edward Bernays (1891–1995), made much of the new 'science' of psychoanalysis that his uncle, Sigmund Freud had created.[31] Writing in 1928, Bernays explained how public relations required both a theoretical and practical understanding of 'the behavioural sciences . . . sociology, social psychology, anthropology, history, etc.'. Scientific knowledge gave the public relations professional the ability to 'control and regiment the masses according to our will without their knowing it'[32] and the modern propagandist studies 'the material with which he is working in the spirit of the laboratory'.[33]

Bernays saw the social system as a machine that could and should be run by specialists. Human desires were 'the steam which makes the social machine work' and, properly controlled, the public would act 'as if actuated by the pressure of a button'.[34] This co-ordination by technicians was necessary because the public is incapable of rational thought, and therefore of self-government. 'The herd' likes to follow the advice or example of a trusted authority figure. Failing that, it relies on 'clichés, pat words or images which stand for a whole group of ideas or experiences'.[35] It is pointless to present the facts to the public and expect them to make a reasonable assessment. They must be stampeded in the required direction. And the rational experts in the new field of public relations constituted a new, if self-effacing, elite: 'Those who manipulate this unseen mechanism of society constitute an invisible government which is the true ruling power in our country . . . It is they who pull the wires that control the public mind.'[36]

Bernays' model, of an irrational, bovine herd that must be managed by an enlightened technical elite, drew on and revised models of society in which an aristocracy of talent presides over everyone else. Indeed his ideas can be seen as an attempt to update and legitimate traditional anti-democratic doctrines, and to establish a modern version of Plato's government by philosopher-kings as the only possible form of organization in conditions of industrial modernity. Unlike the neoconservatives who followed him, Bernays does without mathematico-mystical flummery or nostalgia for the classical city-state, but he would presumably have had some sympathy with Socrates' remark in *The Republic* that 'our Rulers will have to employ a great deal of fiction and deceit for the benefit of their subjects'.[37]

Bernays pioneered the use of what he called 'third party authorities' to promote his clients' interests: 'If you can influence the leaders, either with or without their conscious cooperation, you automatically influence the group which they sway'.[38] In the 1920s, Lucky Strike cigarettes used a survey of physicians to promote their claim that the smoke of their brand was 'less irritating'. Philip Morris went as far as to cite 'eminent medical authorities' for claims about its products, while a competitor boasted that 'more doctors smoke Camels than any other cigarette'.[39] Corporations continue to work hard to retain control of the scientific agenda. Between 1998 and 2005, ExxonMobil gave $16 million to forty-three groups that 'manufacture uncertainty about the danger posed by global warming.'[40] Corporations also continue to contribute heavily to the funding of business-friendly think tanks and non-profit organizations. Pro-business policies sound much better coming from disinterested experts and distinguished scholars.[41]

Edward Bernays began his career as a theatrical promoter. But he and the other public relations specialists learned what propaganda could achieve in the context of the First World War: 'It was, of course, the astounding success of propaganda during the war that opened the eyes of the intelligent few in all departments of life to the possibilities of regimenting the public mind'.[42] The state and private sectors have shared ideas and personnel ever since – Bernays' ambition for push-button control is surely echoed in the CIA's search for 'hot button issues' in its anti-Sandinista campaign. At Abu Ghraib prison, outside Baghdad, a team of interrogators from a company called CACI played an important, if under-reported role, in the treatment of Iraqi prisoners captured during the US–UK invasion of Iraq. The company's website boasts that 'CACI International Inc provides the IT and network solutions needed to prevail in today's new era of defense, intelligence and e-government.' Its British subsidiary provides 'a combination of data, software and consultancy to help you market your products and services more effectively to the right consumers.' CACI's websites don't go into detail about the information-management methods they brought to bear in Abu Ghraib, but Francis Bacon would doubtless have found them fascinating.

When asked why the White House waited until September 2002 before it started to talk about the need to disarm Iraq, Chief of Staff Andrew Card explained that 'from a marketing point of view, you don't introduce new products in August'.[43] In the same month, White House Communications Director Dan Bartlett announced that the same team that had run the public relations side of the war in Afghanistan would manage the campaign against Iraq: 'We're getting the band together', as he put it.[44] Sure enough, until what were intended to be the final scenes of American triumph and Iraqi jubilation in May 2003, their work metastasized through the news and entertainment media. The methods of commercial promotion combined with traditional propaganda techniques to create a super blockbuster called 'Operation Iraqi Freedom'.

While the PR industry uses rational techniques, and finds scientific intermediaries extremely useful, it aims above all to promote its clients' agendas. In 1997 the chairman and general manager of Hill and Knowlton, a company that played a key role in building public support for America's first Gulf War in 1990–91, explained that 'sometimes you have to scare people into action'.[45] The public relations expert, when necessary, undermines the public capacity for reasoned judgement. Under certain circumstances, he or she rationally excites public irrationality in order to promote the interests of the client. There may or may not be some justification for this, but the public relations industry nevertheless poses a very grave 'threat to reason'. It is extremely strange that we do not concentrate on their activities when discussing the Enlightenment in the modern era.

The corporations control much of the $430 billion dollars spent annually worldwide on advertising.[46] This communications effort includes a great deal of outright deception and misinformation. The character of advertisers is systematically misrepresented – while most of them are amoral platforms for maximizing shareholder value, they claim to have human qualities that deserve respect and recognition. Advertising also seeks to invest products with qualities and powers that they do not and cannot have. Every method of associative magic and emotional manipulation is used to increase consumption of the products advertised. Advertisers promote consumption itself as the way to self-realization; they celebrate and enforce the conventions of fashion, and they take advantage of our desire to belong by insinuating that the correct purchase decisions can bring status and happiness. The methods used by advertisers are particularly effective among children, who cannot give their informed consent, and young people, who are emotionally vulnerable and inexperienced. Advertising promotes the use of products that are downright dangerous, including alcohol, tobacco and fast food, and it does so in an environment largely leached of impartial information. Industry as a whole constantly agitates for more opportunities to reach the public, and is often helped by the state in this work. For years the American government has sought to overturn the European ban on consumer advertising for prescription drugs, for example.

By and large, the media take it as an uncontroversial given that the corporation can and does behave in an enlightened manner towards its employees and the wider public. Most media groups are themselves large corporations and they can usually be relied upon to support an agenda from which they themselves stand to benefit. Whether media groups are 'liberal' or 'conservative', they are extremely likely to favour trade liberalization and a *laissez-faire* approach to international capital movements as divisions within transnational corporations. In 1994 the *Washington Post* strongly supported the passage of a bill that would establish the World Trade

Organization (WTO) as an institution with the power to override the US government. The same bill included a provision worth more than a billion dollars to a cellphone company in which the newspaper's parent company had a 70 per cent stake.[47] Those few major media groups that do not have a straightforwardly commercial character recognize that growth depends on attracting an upscale audience and delivering it to advertisers in a politically uncontroversial editorial context. The editor of the *Guardian* recently commented that 'If I had to choose between occupying a niche on the left or being nearer the centre, whether you display that through your news reporting or your comment or both, I'm more comfortable saying this is an upmarket, serious mainstream newspaper. There's more potential for growth there than taking comfort in political positioning.'[48]

State-controlled media groups can only be as confrontational in their dealings with large corporations as the government of the day will tolerate. Although the state in Britain is careful to respect the formal independence of the BBC, serious opposition to government policy is rare and has serious repercussions for those held responsible. The BBC served faithfully to relay government concerns about weapons of mass destruction to the public prior to the US-UK invasion of Iraq. Once the war was declared over, sceptical reporting about the quality of pre-war intelligence cost the jobs of a reporter, Andrew Gilligan, the BBC's director-general, Greg Dyke, and the chairman of its Board of Governors, Gavyn Davies, all of whom resigned in 2004. In the midst of the confrontation between the government and its broadcaster in the summer of 2003 a Ministry of Defence scientist, David Kelly, had been found dead in the countryside near his home.

Some have argued that, under the conditions of close co-operation between the state and business interests, the media are best understood in terms of a 'propaganda model'. Rather than being primarily concerned with providing reliable and impartial information to the public, the mass media's main task is to 'mobilize support for the special interests that dominate the state and private sector'.[49] In other words, if we are to make a rational assessment of the nature of the media, we must recognize the factors preventing serious dissent from reaching a mass audience on a regular basis. Writing in the late 1980s, Noam Chomsky and Edward Herman listed these factors as follows:

(1) The size, concentrated ownership, owner wealth, and profit orientation of the dominant mass-media firms; (2) Advertising as the primary income source of the mass media; (3) The reliance of the media on information provided by government, business, and 'experts' funded and approved by these primary sources and agents of power; (4) 'Flak' as a means of disciplining the media; (5) 'Anti-communism' as a national religion and control mechanism.[50]

The mainstream media are now much more concentrated in terms of ownership and profit orientation than they were when Chomsky and Herman were writing. Five vast media conglomerates now share sales that were in 1983 divided between fifty separate companies.[51] Advertising remains the primary source of income for the mass media. The media continue to rely on official information and approved experts, to the point where important matters of fact can remain controversial long after the truth has been established beyond any serious doubt; media workers for the most part constantly monitor themselves for excessive contrarian zeal. Business groups and enterprising politicians are always on hand to criticize any failure of self-control by journalists and can usually expect a platform for their views. We have already seen how government 'flak' can take a much more lethal form in modern warfare. As for the last element on the list, strenuous efforts are being made to install the War on Terror or the Long War as a 'new national religion', now that communism can no longer serve a reliable propaganda function.

We don't have to accept the Chomsky–Herman analysis wholesale to recognize that, in light of recent and glaring failures, the mass media cannot provide a tolerably reliable picture of reality. The status of Saddam Hussein's weapons programme and the likely impact of global warming are only two of the most serious examples of this unreliability in matters of critical importance to the public. Many other examples can be cited. The total collapse of the Washington Consensus, which began after the Asian currency crisis and accelerated after Argentina's severe recession of 1999, has barely registered in main stream media outlets that are reluctant to examine the facts uncritically or entertain the views of dissenting economists such as Ha-Joon Chang or Erik Reinert. The stock-market bubble of the late 1990s inflated with much cheerleading and talk of 'new paradigms' in the press. Widespread criminality in the corporate sector in the same period was first ignored and later downplayed by the same media.[52] And these failures can only be explained adequately in terms of the wider institutional context in which they have taken place. A serious inquiry into the world leaves us unable to accept many professionally generated descriptions of that world. From an insistence on what one journalist has called 'spurious balance'[53] to the faithful repetition of official mendacity, media groups consistently fail to describe reality when accurate description interferes with the policy goals of dominant interests. Powerful institutions can usually insist on a fair hearing even when they are being dishonest (most obviously in the run-up to the Iraq invasion). Those who lack power can expect no such fair hearing if they challenge powerful institutions, regardless of their expertise, sincerity and relevant experience[54]. We have to recognize the limitations imposed on journalists as wage-earners and as economic-ally rational beings. An end to tutelage means realizing that we alone, acting as sceptical and independent observers, can discover the world as it is.

The governing coalition of private and state power that does so much to shape and distort descriptions of the world goes by many names – it reaches far beyond the managed oppositions of con-ventional politics and mainstream journalism. It reveals itself in the militarization of corporate language and in the unselfconscious marketing-speak of government officials. It reveals itself in the hopeless absurdities of our law enforcement system and the related, awkward silence about how the global economy works. Something of its synthetic nature is captured in terms like the military–industrial and military–entertainment complex. Within its institutions the Enlightenment is nurtured in its occult form and permitted to flourish, along with a bewildering number of other ideologies.[55] Through a process very like idolatry it has become for many the only defender of Enlightenment. Perhaps Voltaire would have called it *l'infâme*. If we are to call things by their names, then let us call it 'the Monster'.

8

An Enlightened Method

It's not a matter of emancipating truth from every system of power (which would be a chimera, for truth is already power) but of detaching the power of truth from the forms of hegemony, social, economic, and cultural, within which it operates at the present time.

Michel Foucault

We do not for the most part understand the world in which we live. Both the state and the corporation remain mysterious in themselves, and they generate misunderstanding and delusion on a vast scale. Trillions of dollars disappear from reckonings of government departments and the general population is routinely treated as an object to be manipulated. The private sector spends hundreds of billions of dollars making deception both palatable and ubiquitous. To the limited extent that we can grasp the facts in a given context, we find ourselves contradicted by the major media groups. In such circumstances we cannot reasonably claim to live in enlightened times.

Given these circumstances, we have a number of options. We can give up on the idea of Enlightenment and accept that it isn't for us to know what is going on. We can try to live honestly while ignoring the mendacity within which we make our lives. Perhaps that's what most of us do right now. Or we can try to hold on to our enlightened identity while accepting the description of reality offered by the dominant institutions. If we make such a choice, we will become avid for the various forms of Folk Enlightenment.

We will become fearful about the rising tide of irrational and unreasonable forces that threaten the enlightened inheritance, and we will establish an attachment to the culture of Enlightenment through a process of historical re-enactment. While resisting religion or the New Age we'll get to impersonate Voltaire but we will take on faith what we are told by those who wield real power. We will believe the right myths, the ones that people like us believe: myths about the benevolence of state and corporation, about the inevitability of our current arrangements, about human nature and capitalism. We will rage against postmodernists, fundamentalists and practitioners of alternative medicine, but, to an extent that we cannot acknowledge, we will be quite docile. Terrible crimes will be committed by our rulers, with our money, while we stand guard against the dangers of a revived Inquisition or a reanimated Adolf Hitler. Our claims to be enlightened will rest on an anxious refusal to acknowledge our ignorance.

If we can't summon the necessary innocence to believe what we're told, we can embrace the world of power as it stands and seek to find out the truth through the pursuit of economic or political power. We will pretend to believe in public whatever serves our purposes and busy ourselves with the acquisition of secret knowledge. This is the path that some politicians and financiers have taken. It requires that we give up on the Open Enlightenment, on Enlightenment-as-freedom. At best we can adopt a pastoral or therapeutic attitude to those who remain unenlightened; in Socrates' words in the *Republic*, falsehood becomes a kind of medicine administered by the rulers to ensure stability.[2] The pursuit of Enlightenment in secret, as described by Plato, and it has a certain superficial grandeur. But all that stuff about a secret, higher order of reality, a reality that cannot be grasped by lesser minds, after the symposia and the conviviality, it must strike even the most dedicated state intellectual as being philosophically untenable. Still, perhaps the betrayal of philosophy is the price one must pay to become a modern philosopher-king.

Other responses have been proposed. We can retreat from the

world into a life of aesthetic experience. In this vein the cultural critic and scholar Morris Berman has called for a new monastic movement, in which internal exiles from the babble of the entertainment economy will pursue meaningful lives, and preserve the values of Western civilization through the coming Dark Ages.[1] Berman believes that the escape from banality and illusion can only be enjoyed by a tiny minority.[2] As he puts it, 'The day you see David Barsamian on "Larry King Live", you can be sure that alternative radio has lost its edge.' Most of us must be abandoned to the frantic nullity of capitalist modernity. Berman acknowledges that a revived and clarified Enlightenment might come about in due course, but only as a result of historical forces beyond our control, through a 'Great Collapse' of the corporate economy, rather than 'as a result of a "new consciousness", or spirituality, or some form of wilful populist activity':

> [We] are in the grip of structural forces that are the culmination of a certain historical process, so a major change is not likely to be quick or dramatic; but individual shifts in lifeways and values might just possibly act as a wedge that would serve as a counter-weight to the world of schlock, ignorance, social inequality, and mass consumerism that now defines the American landscape. At the very least, these 'new monks', or native expatriates, as one might call them, could provide a kind of record of authentic ways of living that could be preserved and handed down, to resurface later on, during healthier times.[3]

Alternatively, we can build an independent, if hopelessly outmatched, opposition to the deception around us. The American scholar and author Curtis White, calls for a self-consciously anti-corporate caste to escape from the continual dulling of mainstream culture and build an alternative space in which the work of the imagination is somehow incorporated into social life. He finds grounds for qualified optimism in the coalition-building of the political and artistic avant-gardes, between, for example, environmental activists and the McSweeney's publishing operation. 'They will fail in the short run, but they will, I hope, experience the imagination's state of grace in the process'.[4] This is a model of resistance that traces itself back to the bohemian tradition of the nineteenth century. White hopes that something can be saved, at least for a minority with the will and the wit to escape from the mainstream. What he suggests is a variation on the idea of the heroic, and heroic because totally committed, artist-as-rebel. But neither internal exile nor the creation of confrontational artistic cultures entirely suffice as enlightened responses to the present moment. Berman and White suggest approaches that either defer meaningful political action to some post-lapsarian future, or substitute agitation by a tiny minority of political and artistic provocateurs for a politics of material transformation. Any bohemian opposition is bound to be overwhelmed, its achievements repackaged as commodities, and its most successful figures paid into submission.

The revolutionary tradition of the nineteenth century pins its hopes on the creation of a political vanguard party that will educate the masses away from the enchantments of state and corporate power towards total freedom. But such parties are always in danger of decaying into yet another betrayal of the Enlightenment that reproduces the state's trickery in miniature. In a world of total revolutionary commitment, the truth is welcome as a resource to be exploited. But the unenlightened masses are not ready for the whole truth. Lies and deception must form part of the arsenal of the revolution. For it is the transformation of the world, rather than the work of accurate description, that preoccupies the revolutionary. Faced with a deceitful enemy in a struggle to the death, the revolution can only be defended by an equal and opposite mendacity. This is not to say that the revolutionary turn is always mistaken, only that it entails the abandonment of truth as an overriding consideration. In practical terms, the revolutionary party in Britain and the United States promises only frustration and failure. The British and American states have time and again demonstrated their virtuosity in capturing and manipulating revolutionary movements. Tiny revolutionary parties provide valuable educational opportunities for those who want to grow up to be professional politicians (European social democrats often acknowledge a Maoist or Stalinist past with a rueful smile. In Britain, New Labour would have been impossible without the contribution of former student radicals. Even in the United States many neo-conservatives came from the Trotskite left). But revolutionary groups have, to a large extent, become fly-traps for youthful idealism.

Bohemian, monastic and revolutionary responses to the current moment have in common the desire to preserve, if only for a minority, a unitary identity. Whether we withdraw from mainstream culture or place ourselves in uncompromising opposition to it, the aim is always to preserve a unified and authentic self. The artistic agitator who revolts against corporate values and somehow creates a life outside of the hallucinatory mainstream culture does so in order to maintain his or her integrity. Even the secret revolutionary leading a double life is *really* a revolutionary; in this way he or she transcends day-to-day immersion in the world of established institutional power, retaining an unsullied secret core. This ambition for total integration of the self, this anxious longing to be free of anxiety, stands in the way of Enlightenment.

REVIVING THE KANTIAN ENLIGHTENMENT, OR A FISHBOWL FOR LEVIATHAN

It is difficult to get a man to understand something when his salary depends on his not understanding.
Upton Sinclair, I, Candidate for Governor:
And How I Got Licked (1935)

We have already looked at Kant's description of Enlightenment as the end of intellectual tutelage. For Kant, adult understanding is possible only in the context of a public realm in which individuals meet, share ideas and examine social arrangements in the light of reason. Enlightenment inheres in our decision to set aside our 'private' roles and identities as employees, albeit temporarily, and to inquire into the nature of things without fear of censure, or hope of advantage:

> By the public use of one's reason I understand the use which a person makes of it as a scholar before the reading public. Private use I call that which one may make of it in a particular civil post or office which is intrusted to him.[7]

Kant's idea of an objective public realm, in which we approach controversies not as self-interested partisans but as disinterested researchers, suggests how we might reclaim Enlightenment as a matter of lived experience. It is not a question of aspiring to total Enlightenment, but of attending to reality for its own sake, without hope of reward, for some part of our time. If we set aside the pursuit of personal advantage, we gain some measure of freedom, as much freedom as is compatible with our remaining human. Given that we do not fully understand the political and economic context in which we live, and that the legitimacy of our current guardians rests on their continued control of our understanding in this respect, it is here that the most pressing work of Enlightenment stands to be done.

It is an orderly investigation into the constitution of human reality, rather than a confrontation between faith and reason, that captures Kant's understanding of Enlightenment. Enlightenment understood in this sense, as an inquiry into what is the case, precedes and makes possible a campaign against injustice that is intellectually attractive because it is also a campaign against deception. No institution to which we relate as employees, be it a corporation, a department of state, a university or an NGO, can provide a venue for truly disinterested public debate. All institutions are private spaces – all too real, but arenas in which we are caught up in the logic of competition, greed and fear. Our lives outside these institutions continue to be private, in Kant's sense of the word, if we allow them to be governed by institutional (usually state and corporate) values. A 'private' life given over entirely to recreation and consumption does not lead to liberation from the life of work, but to the end of Enlightenment. Once we recognize that our status as employees of private institutions compromises our claims to Enlightenment, we can set about self-consciously creating a public body of knowledge. This work will permit us to address each other as equals and to escape temporarily from the business of getting and spending.[5]

This work, the work of Enlightenment, will not be conducted in isolation from the state–corporate system. Expertise from our 'private' lives as well as the products of the information economy can be brought into public research and redeployed in pursuit of disinterested knowledge. Rather than operating as a marginal alternative in which certain kinds of symbolic gestures and sacrifices must be made to secure acceptance – the depressingly persistent idea that radical sincerity has something to do with clothing and hair-styles – the work of public inquiry runs alongside private institutional life. No individual is expected to identify with it entirely. As human beings we have conflicting impulses and cannot remain reliably impartial. Making a contribution to this kind of research depends on our ability to learn about the world, to make sense of that knowledge, and to persuade others of our interpretations.

In such work, authority is distributed among the participants who together settle on descriptions of reality that best capture the relevant facts. Instead of an audience enlightened by the intellectual we have a society of equals; instead of peer review we have open review by the public. Expertise in a particular area might provide valuable skills and useful background knowledge; doctors might concentrate on inquiry into public health and the political economy of science, accountants might take a particular interest in the structure of global and especially offshore finance. But private expertise does not guarantee assent by a wider public. A claim earns authority only insofar as it is persuasive to a disinterested public. If hundreds or thousands of people, experts and amateurs, have agreed on a common account, the fact of consensus, rather than some other form of prestige, gives others a reason to pay attention. In this way we transcend our self-interest, not because we as individuals achieve an entirely unbiased point of view, but because the outcome of our common inquiry will outstrip the agenda of any one individual. It is the process of open review by people who have only a very general stake in any one area of inquiry that creates a commonly agreed body of knowledge. Such a body of knowledge will eventually surpass all other possible accounts – including the products of the state and corporation – in the eyes of thousands, and then of millions, of people worldwide. The fact of agreement on the grand scale provides a means by which the power of truth can be detached in a substantial way from other forms of power. Only such public descriptions can create a fishbowl for the leviathan in whose belly so many of us spend our days. Those who hold other forms of power and who ignore such a body of public knowledge, will pay a heavy, perhaps unbearable, price: they will become universally ridiculous.

Of course what we produce will not be 'perfect knowledge' or 'perfectly unbiased' – disinterested researchers can agree all but unanimously on an account that is untrue, and must remain alive to the possibility. But what we seek is not a philosophical destination but a starting point for political action. To repeat, I am not pretending that it is ever entirely possible for us as individuals to achieve total scholarly impartiality – or that we will be able to discover the 'truly universal truth'. I do think, however, that as individuals we can assess evidence and information with a certain degree of impartiality, and that collectively we can pool and synthesize the results of our work and thereby come ever closer to an adequate description of political reality. A programme of inquiry conducted outside the market will be superior to any possible commercial alternative, since it will not be forced to down play or exaggerate certain features of that reality in order to protect established institutional interests.

Most of us cannot and will not sacrifice our careers and the welfare of our families for the abstract demands of universal truth and justice. But we are nevertheless confused and distressed by the contradictions inherent in the state and corporate bureaucracies of Britain and America. We are encouraged to believe that in our working lives we belong to a 'community', even a 'family', that demands more than the fulfilment of contractual obligations. The dominant institutions pretend to be our friends, and our continued survival in a corporate context depends on our ability to reciprocate, or at least to make a good pretence of doing so. But they are not and cannot be our friends. They relate to us as dictators, as incarnations of Adorno's nightmare Enlightenment – we are things to be used and discarded as appropriate. Our working lives are conducted in an atmosphere of straight-faced but blatant mendacity. Self-consciously public research allows us to recognize and make sense of this mendacity and register fully our complicity in it. In our role as public researchers, however, we replace profit with truth as the objective of inquiry. In such a way we come to understand ourselves as economic actors, and the marketplace itself, more fully. An active acceptance of our dual nature as private and public agents holds out the prospect of a world transformed. As individuals we will see the world afresh, under the conditions of a more thoroughgoing honesty. Collectively we will describe the world in ways that make political action morally necessary and therefore politically possible.

The dream is not of escape, through promotion, consumption or internal exile, but of comprehension. Once we meet as public researchers and begin the work of understanding the times in which we live, the state and the corporation cease to be sources of irresolvable anxiety and swindling hope. They become available to thought as we allow ourselves to think in terms that transcend their internal logic. Neither loyalty nor the profit motive can shield them from us once we begin to subject them to public inquiry, for both are subordinated to publicly accessible criteria of truth. The state and the corporation fall under our power, to the extent that we are able to stand outside them. This is surely what we mean when we talk of 'comprehension' – it is the process by which we abstract ourselves from our own circumstances, the better to grasp the world. We do not have to renounce our private identities as employees. But we must recognize that the sum of our private identities does not constitute the full expression of our humanity.

Such a move requires that we give up a certain regime of

pleasures. It means giving up the illusion or the hope of an integrated life in which the tension between private interests and public inquiry is finally resolved. We have to stop imagining that we deserve to be believed because of our educational attainments, our institutional position or our personal integrity. We will risk being effectively contradicted by those who we could confidently dismiss in other contexts on the grounds that they were naive or extremist (or female, or black, or homosexual, or rich, or poor . . .). Faced with matters of fact, we can have no lasting refuge in authority. Enlightenment is only possible when we are prepared to set aside our status as experts, or rather when we recognize that we have to earn that status repeatedly before a disinterested public who do not care who we are in our private capacity.

This process will be particularly difficult for those intellectuals who like to think of themselves as educators of the otherwise confused masses. At the would-be stirring finale of *Where Have All the Intellectuals Gone* (2004), Frank Furedi declares that 'we can wage a battle for the hearts and minds of the public', which seems to me to exhibit precisely the temptation that intellectuals will have to set aside.[6] Talk of 'hearts and minds' belongs in counter-insurgency warfare doctrine, it has nothing to contribute to a resurgent Enlightenment. The public is not a native population to be won over by intellectuals parachuted in by a higher authority. The public is the only possible instigator and defender of enlightened progress in the long term.

We will have to dispense with another conceit popular with intellectuals, what might be called the Myth of Jefferson. Kant and Bacon, with their monarchism and their Christianity, are problematic emblems for Enlightenment. The great sceptic and humanist Thomas Jefferson seems a much more congenial model. He was, after all, a dashing enemy of religious cant, the proud author of the Declaration of Independence, and the United States' third president. Surely he, rather than the loyal subjects of tyrannical princes, should provide us with our model of enlightened adulthood? But the educated classes in Britain and America have far more in common with Kant and Bacon than with Jefferson. Though we might like to imagine ourselves to be autonomous free-thinkers, fearlessly willing to speak truth to power, for the most part we depend on powerful institutions for prestige and material well-being. In such circumstances we deceive ourselves if we imagine that we are able simply to integrate our duty to the public pursuit of truth and our private responsibilities to our patrons. This deception extends to our attitude towards Enlightenment itself, if it leads us to rail against opponents that have little or no sway over our career prospects, and to ignore the threat to reason posed by our employers.

We cannot draw on the material and emotional comfort of a world of secure and pliant possessions. Rather, we are hemmed in by, and derive sustenance from, institutions and individuals that themselves cannot attach an absolute value to the truth. In such circumstances, Kant's division of the public and the private becomes a matter of deep relevance to us. Serious political action looks a great deal like the duty to truth outlined by him in the 1780s. As the employees of states and corporations we cannot allow ourselves the luxury of imagining that the important truths will be self-evident and unthreatening to all but religious fanatics and super-modern champions of unreason. Instead we must recognize that we exist in a state of permanent tension between what is required of us in our social and economic roles and what our decision for truth impels us to know. Old-fashioned Kant, wrestling with the competing claims of his king and his conscience, has much more to say to us today than the dashing and magnificent Jefferson. We are, if we are honest with ourselves, place-holders not plantation-owners.

Kant recognized that we can, as scholars, criticize claims we must defend as employees. But he also saw that our final duty is to the truth as discovered through public inquiry, not to the institutions that employ us, insofar as we aim to become in some substantial sense enlightened. Exactly how we manage the tension between our public and private roles is by no means clear – the lack of clarity is only one of many sources of discomfort in the actual experience, as opposed to the fantasy, of Enlightenment. Enlightenment resides above all in recognizing our own ambiguous relationship with truth and with other forms of power. We are formed in part by our relationship with power – effective political action will require that we give up more than our illusions about the external world. We must also abandon illusions about ourselves.

And just as we give up the illusion of Jeffersonian autonomy, we must also give up the pleasure of believing that we already understand the world. Almost all of us are as confused and puffed-up with error as the students of Aristotle and Galen who so infuriated Bacon. General consent and the authority of 'men counted great in philosophy' continue to hold us back, 'as by a kind of enchantment', from progress in understanding the world.[7] It is a subject too great to consider here, but Bacon's flight from theory towards the facts of the world has a good deal to teach us about how we might pursue a programme of public inquiry. Rather than rushing to concoct theoretical accounts of political economy, perhaps we should concentrate on establishing with greater precision what has happened in the past and what is happening now.

THE METHOD OF ENLIGHTENMENT

The outlines of a programme of enlightened inquiry begin to emerge. Public research motivated by a disinterested commitment to truth provides an idealized model of the enlightened method. The subject matter of Enlightenment is found in matters of material fact, rather than theological or metaphysical speculation. This at any rate is what I have argued, and sought to demonstrate, in previous chapters. Collective authorship and open review provide the means by which the work of individuals takes on a wider political significance, the mechanism by which individual Enlightenment fuels general progress.

The free software movement shows how great collaborative endeavours can take place beyond the reach of conventional, institutional power, beyond both the state and the corporation. As pioneered by the great engineer and programmer Richard Stallman, the GPL (General Public License), for example, allows recipients of a programme to alter and distribute it to others, on condition that they pass on the same freedom to subsequent users. GPL software is protected by copyright and so later copies or revisions cannot escape the original terms of the licence. In this way GPL software cannot be enclosed in software that is itself not released under the terms of the GPL. There are many other free software licences which impose slightly different terms from the ones in the GPL. Almost all the software used to send and receive emails on the internet was made available under the terms of one or other of these free software licences. The Firefox web browser and the Linux operating system were also released on a free software licence.[8]

Free software demonstrates that royalties are not necessary to stimulate research, even in the realm of product development. The success of free software should make us optimistic that we can develop a free information movement, in which the goal is not the creation of a piece of software, but individual and collective liberation. If hundreds of programmers can collaborate to create the Linux operating system, without any immediate financial incentives, we should be optimistic about the viability of a free information movement. The proliferation of free software licences and the history of collaboration on the great free software projects both offer useful clues to how public research might develop. Subtle and apparently trivial differences in method have had a decisive impact on the success of individual projects. The same is likely to be true for public research projects into political economy.[9]

Different approaches to this work of public research can be tried, and they will either attract collaborators or fail to do so and be abandoned. Communities of inquiry can assemble around particular events, institutions, historical periods and so on. They can publish their findings in anything from short, non-technical abstracts to book-length articles for academic-readers. They can produce audio and video documentaries and books intended for a wide readership that can be published commercially. The results can be integrated and reused without the need for a central organizing authority. New technology provides the means by which information can be shared on a scale never before possible and it allows us to manipulate and refine this information with great sophistication. Forms of collective authorship can be developed using interactive technology. Something like the GPL can be employed to ensure that authorship is protected while the products of research remain freely available. This is not to confuse cyberspace with some uncomplicatedly emancipated zone of engagement, but rather to emphasize that we have unprecedented opportunities to subject claims about the world to open review in a manner that bypasses existing institutional power. This might sound unrealistic or even utopian. But it is already happening, and happening on a massive scale. Web journalism and blogs are already exposing the vulnerability of the mainstream media to competition from non-professional searchers. Wikipedia demonstrates the superiority of collective authorship over older, copyright and royalty-driven methods for generating reference material. A body of collaboratively authored material like Sourcewatch (http://www.sourcewatch.org)[13] provides a model for similar projects and a venue where we can join the work of public inquiry right now. Enlightenment does not necessarily require that we create new zones of participatory research, but that we join, expand and develop those that already exist.

As with the free software movement, private interests will of course seek to profit from the work done by unpaid researchers, seeing it as common land to be enclosed and exploited for commercial gain; indeed corporate control of the internet means that corporations stand to profit in the immediate term from an upsurge in public research. And the state will do what it can to control or minimize the impact of public research; those striving for information dominance can hardly be expected to ignore the creation of a body of knowledge that disrupts their activities. But in this environment states and corporations will be unable to call on the normal punishments and rewards. How can one bribe everyone, or threaten people who have nothing to lose? Together we can challenge established, allegedly enlightened descriptions of the world and propose in their place openly generated, and openly reviewed, descriptions of our own. Gradually myth will lose its hold on the general population. This is not the lifeboat for a few sensitive souls envisaged by Morris Berman and Curtis White, it is the means by which the ship itself might be saved.

The notion of Enlightenment as a programme of disinterested inquiry into the world brings with it serious dangers. We will almost certainly make disastrous mistakes, collectively and as individuals. Attempting to make independent use of our reason exposes us to error and to ridicule. Without the support of certain secure categories of thought we are almost bound to stumble. To change the metaphor, after years in the darkness, a little light can be blinding. While Kant was optimistic that error would be temporary, not everyone recovers from the shock of independence of mind. Some will remain trapped in all-explaining conspiracies that are seductive precisely because they capture, while disastrously distorting, important elements of truth. But we must include the secret, the disreputable and the seemingly insane in any adequate programme of inquiry, even though to do so is to risk obsession.

This, then, is Enlightenment. It is, I think, an Enlightenment that Kant would have recognized, in that it depends on trying to establish a distinction between ourselves as employees and as impartial researchers. Kant believed that enlightened and therefore legitimate authority would welcome the emergence of an enlightened public sphere. Perhaps admiration for Frederick the Great influenced his judgement, perhaps he had no choice but to be optimistic, and to locate the substance of his Enlightenment in religious matters, where his king's enlightened credentials were impeccable. We cannot afford Kant's optimism. There are risks and costs associated with the decision for Enlightenment.

We must also be clear-eyed about the reaction that unencumbered inquiry into the world will provoke from the guardians of the established order. The risks we run and the insights we gain will be met with ridicule and worse. But while we are in one sense self-interested agents in a knowledge economy, the Enlightenment described by Kant, the Open Enlightenment, allows us to live at least part of the time as truth-loving individuals. Seen in this way, Enlightenment once more becomes a route to universal emancipation from superstition and error. As part-time public researchers we stop being a passive audience to be addressed by an enlightened elite. We become the authors of our own Enlightenment.

Conclusion

My aim in this book has not been to deny that irrational beliefs can create real dangers. Religious dogma plays an important role in justifying terror attacks on civilian populations. Young men convinced that their actions will be rewarded in heaven have launched attacks in both the United States and Britain in recent years. But faith in the benevolence and veracity of the state has made possible far more carnage in the years since 2001. Whether they believed that Western troops would be welcomed as liberators or that Saddam Hussein's weapons of mass destruction posed an unacceptable threat, secular intellectuals should have taken greater trouble to establish whether their own beliefs were founded on 'the assurance of things hoped for, the conviction of things unseen'.

It is true that in much of the world, religion continues to act as a barrier to understanding. In the Middle East, those liberals and socialists still alive long to see an end to the powerful amalgam of religious and cultural fantasy that underpins the oil-rich regimes of the Gulf. But many, perhaps most, of the democratic reformers in the Middle East are also devout Muslims. They see no more need to renounce their religion than did the Christian socialists of the early twentieth century. Their vision of a just society does not require an end to religious faith; Mahatma Gandhi and Martin Luther King both show how religion can inform and substantiate hope for peaceful progress. To confuse the struggle for justice in the Middle East with the struggle against religion is to give up any serious attempt to understand social and political reality for the pleasures of the Folk Enlightenment. Clear-eyed inquiry cannot help but notice that Britain has shored up religious monarchy in the region since the First World War and that radical Islam has consistently collaborated with US power since 1945. If we want to defeat 'fascism with an Islamic face', we ought to begin by registering Western state complicity in creating and maintaining it.

In Britain and the US itself, the attempt to put a showdown between faith and reason at the centre of the concept of Enlightenment looks even more misconceived. Though there are some people who challenge science and reason from avowedly faith-based or openly irrational positions, they are few in number and they enjoy little sustained support from the wider public. When such people seek to intimidate scientists they must be met with the full rigour of the law, and when they seek to introduce religious dogma where it is inappropriate they should of course be resisted. But we need to retain a sense of proportion in these matters. Religion fuses with other forms of power in the United States as elsewhere and, for the most part, religious leaders are happy to sell their followers to the politicians that pay them the most. George W. Bush's career shows how blather about knowing Christ and family values is backed up by worldly rewards for the Evangelical leadership. By any sensible measure, Evangelical politics has been a ludicrous failure: tens of millions of votes have gone to candidates who have largely ignored them. We can take the religious right seriously without pretending that it is the most pressing threat to Enlightenment at the present time.

Writing about the British Enlightenment, Roy Porter noted that 'Enlightened activism always involved clashing interests, and its elastic ideological resources could be deployed for radical ends or equally by sections of the propertied, plutocratic and polite against those they sought to discredit, convert, or marginalize.'[1] If this is true in the eighteenth century, it is surely true in the twenty-first. I have argued that, in the nominally enlightened West, the substantial fight for Enlightenment must now take place between Open and Occult Enlightenment. This requires that we cease to be entranced by the struggle with an unreason willing to declare itself that we find in the productions of the Folk Enlightenment. Enlightenment as a moral project, a self-conscious commitment to material improvement on the basis of open inquiry, struggles in the West with an Occult Enlightenment, in which knowledge serves other forms of power – inquiry takes place in secret without moral restraint. This other Enlightenment focuses on personal transformation and the exultation of powerful institutions, especially the state and the corporation. It is ambitious for total power, and therefore for total knowledge, and it is in love with secrecy. It is happy to promote irrationality and misunderstanding among those whom it wishes to control; it is voracious for data at that same time that it radiates deception.

The early Enlightenment of the seventeenth century sought to solve the mysteries of the physical world, to make creation obedient to the will of man. This meant above all extricating our understanding from religious superstition and scholastic pretension in what was, for all its limitations, a moral project, an attempt to improve the condition of mankind. This project has been triumphantly, and sometimes disastrously, successful, realizing itself both in longer life expectancy and industrialized murder. Kant hoped to extend Enlightenment into the personal sphere. His task was to explain how unlimited freedom of inquiry might be compatible with social order under conditions of monarchy. Our task is to continue his work under conditions of secular democracy and corporate capitalism, in a political system that does not depend for its legitimacy on religious authority, but on claims about the nature of reality. This does not mean establishing a science of human nature; it means disenchanting ourselves about how society functions in particular contexts. The decision for Enlightenment reaches outward to comprehend society's dominant institutions, the state and the corporation, and inward to recognition of our participation in their workings.

Enlightenment is difficult. There is much to find that has been hidden, and more in plain view that is misunderstood. Yet only a world more fully understood can be transformed. As we face the prospect of permanent war and accelerating environmental collapse, we cannot afford to delude ourselves about what it means now to dare to know. Enlightenment is dangerous. As we begin the work of knowing the world without restraint we will be forced to address subjects that threaten vertigo;[2] to take seriously the fact that secrecy disguises and distorts the nature and actions of the most powerful actors in our society is terribly disorientating. We are almost bound to stumble and so lend plausibility to the efforts of the state and corporation to convince others that opposition to them is a form of mental illness. Furthermore, broad-based, patient inquiry that abstains from state and commercial organization holds out some prospect of success. The tyrannical and the unjust cannot be expected to sit idly by until they are unmasked and removed from their positions of power and prestige. If we work carefully for truth as public-minded researchers, we will quite soon come to pose a threat, a rationally grounded threat, to the current system.

Public research conducted without prejudice might conclude that somehow homeopaths and postmodern academics really do pose the most serious threats to the values of the Enlightenment, or that bin Laden in his hideout really is a plausible successor to Joseph Stalin. And if we do begin the work of understanding the Occult Enlightenment, it is possible, even likely, that the Monster will respond with ever more desperate violence, ever more dazzling special effects. The hope of a world safe for truth might die as the established powers move to repress by force what they can no longer control through the tyranny of opinion. But it is also possible that we will understand the world and ourselves more quickly than our guardians can frighten us, that we will make good on the promise of Enlightenment, and that our daring to know will at last make another world possible.

It is up to us to find out.

Acknowledgements

I would like to thank Jake Osborne, Tamasin Cave, Larry Sieden-
top, Joel Bakan, Philip Augar and Sally Brett for reading and
commenting on early versions of the text. Whatever flaws the
book may still have, it has been greatly improved by their help and
advice. I am doubly grateful to Sally Brett, who, as my flatmate,
allowed me to commandeer her computer (and the study) for long
periods of time. Without her generosity and tolerance this book
would not have happened. Fiamma Montagu, Fabrice and Alexei
Boltho, Rebecca Fox, Jörg Hensgen and Canan Gunduz helped me
to organize my thoughts and encouraged me in various ways to
write the best book I could. Thanks especially to Rebecca Urang
for her thoughtful contributions.

I am very grateful to Caroline Pretty for her work copy editing
the text on a very tight schedule. Thanks to everyone at Verso for
their hard work. Finally, I'd like to acknowledge my very considerable debt to Tom Penn. His tact and acuity have saved me from
innumerable blunders, and he has taught me a good deal about what
it means to be an editor.

This book is inspired by the work of public inquiry taking place
now throughout the world. If *The Threat to Reason* encourages
others to join this effort, then I will have achieved something, as
much as anyone could hope for.

Notes

INTRODUCTION: WHY ENLIGHTENMENT? WHY NOW?

1. 'President Bush discusses Iraq policy at Whitehall Palace in London', 19 November 2003. In the speech Bush also refers to Lord Shaftesbury, Wilberforce and the Royal Navy. http://www.state.gov/p/eur/rls/rm/2003/26360.htm

2. ' "Clash about civilisations" speech', 21 March 2006. *http://www.number10.-gov.uk/output/Page9224.asp* (accessed 16 February 2007). According to Blair we face a clash *about* civilization, rather than a clash *of* civilizations: elements in all cultures embrace modernity while others reject it. Blair seems to want to bomb anyone who shows insufficient enthusiasm for progress. Presumably an exception can be made in the national interest for major clients of the British arms industry.

3. Victor Davis Hanson, 'Traitors to the Enlightenment', *National Review Online*, 2 October 2006. *http://victorhanson.com/articles/hanson100306.html* (accessed 16 February 2007).

4. Of course many of those described as neoconservatives reject the Enlightenment. Speaking about Leo Strauss, one of the key figures in neoconservatism, Irving Kristol has said that 'what made him so controversial within the academic community was his disbelief in the Enlightenment dogma that "the truth will make men free".' Kristol himself has said that 'There are different kinds of truths for different kinds of people . . . There are truths appropriate for children; truths that are appropriate for students; truths that are appropriate for educated adults; and truths that are appropriate for highly educated adults, and the notion that there should be one set of truths available to everyone is a modern democratic fallacy. It doesn't work.' Quoted in Brian Doherty, 'Origin of the Specious', *Reason Magazine*, July 1997.

5. Milton Friedman, 'Please reread your Adam Smith', *Wall Street Journal*, 24 June 1987.

6. 'Rescuing environmentalism', *The Economist*, 21 April 2005. In 2006 'Adam Smith' was mentioned in *The Economist* on average once every four weeks.

7. Dick Taverne, *The March of Unreason* (Oxford: Oxford University Press, 2005), p.15.
8. 'Reality Wars', *New Scientist*, 8 October 2005.
9. Nick Cohen, 'Don't know your left from your right?', *Observer*, 21 January 2007.
10. For more about Enlightenment and blackmail, see Michel Foucault's essay *What is Enlightenment?* collected in Michel Foucault, *Ethics* (London: Allen Lane, 1997), pp.303–19.
11. Friedrich Nietzsche, *Twilight of the Idols, or How to Philosophise with a Hammer* (Oxford: Oxford University Press 1998).

CHAPTER 1: THE PARTY OF MODERNITY

1. Some also seek to distinguish between a pragmatic and capitalist British Enlightenment and a utopian and terrorist French version. See, for example, Gertrude Himmelfarb, *The Roads to Modernity* (New York: Knopf, 2004). Gordon Brown, the prominent British politician, has quoted Himmelfarb approvingly.
2. See Greg Grandin, *Empire's Workshop* (New York: Metropolitan 2006) for an excellent short history of Latin America.
3. This summary of the 'economic orthodoxy' of 'market states' comes from Philip Bobbitt, *The Shield of Achilles: War, Peace and the Course of History* (New York: Knopf, 2002), p.667. Bobbitt also speaks of the need to reduce subsidies and to remove restrictions on trade. To describe this new orthodoxy, Bobbitt draws on the 'fundamental assumptions that Margaret Thatcher and Tony Blair urged for Britain and that Bill Clinton and George W. Bush urged for the United States'. Clinton's campaign rhetoric in particular stressed the need for labour flexibility and tight controls on public spending in a world of unrestricted capital mobility.
4. An excellent summary of the propaganda for unfettered, 'democratic' markets can be found in Thomas Frank's *One Market Under God* (London: Random House, 2001).
5. Quoted in Roger Kerr's 1998 speech to the Chartered Institute of Corporate Management in New Zealand.
6. Adam Smith Institute website, http://www.adamsmith.org/about/
7. *House of Commons Hansard Debates*, 5 July 1989.
8. *Adam Smith Goes to Moscow: A Dialogue on Radical Reform* by Walter Adams and James W. Brock was published in 1993 by Princeton University Press.
9. Vaclav Klaus, 'The Adam Smith address: Adam Smith's legacy and economic transformation of Czechoslovakia', *Business Economics* January 1993.
10. The interview with Gaidar is available online at *http://www.pbs.org/wgbh/commandingheights/shared/minitextlo/int_yegorgaidar.html* (accessed 16 February 2007).
11. Adam Smith, *The Wealth of Nations* (London: Penguin, 1997), p.119.
12. Noam Chomsky, *Understanding Power* (New York: The New Press, 2002),

pp.221–2. Chomsky's comments were recorded either in 1989 or between 1993 and 1996 (see ibid., p.177).

13. See, for example, Dan Plesch, 'Corporate social responsibility: questions of equality before the law, property rights and deregulation', *Accountancy Business and the Public Interest*, 2005, vol. 4, no. 2. Plesch argues that limited liability acts as a form of unequal protection for shareholders that should be a prime target for mainstream critics of government regulation; his logic is very difficult to fault.

14. See, for example, Anatol Lieven's article 'History is not bunk', *Prospect*, October 1998.

15. Smith, op. cit., p.117.

16. Smith, op. cit., p.232.

17. For example, John Gray wrote that 'a single global market is the Enlightenment project of a universal civilization in what is likely to be its final form'. Cited in Brink Lindsey, 'A Gray World', *Reason Magazine*, July 1999.

18. Anthony Giddens, 'The Reith Lectures revisited: lecture 1', 10 November 1999.

19. Giddens, op.cit. The dream of the Enlightenment philosophers Giddens refers to is one of a world increasingly subject to rational control.

20. David Harvey, *A Brief History of Neoliberalism* (Oxford: Oxford University Press, 2005), p.154.

21. Harvey, op. cit., p.154.

22. See Joseph Stiglitz, *Globalization and its Discontents* (London: Penguin, 2002) for a more detailed account of the excesses of IMF-lead liberalization in the 1990s. As a Nobel Prize-winner and former Chief Economist at the World Bank, Stiglitz has a unique authority in these matters. But it is worth remembering that his critique of economic orthodoxy was several years behind that of the anti-globalization movement.

23. Harvey, op. cit., p.17.

24. Peter Beinart, *The New Republic Online*, 13 September 2001, quoted in 'Globalization, disobedience and the rule of law', by Professor Leslie Green, *http://www.law.nyu.edu/kingsburyb/fall06/globalization/papers/Leslie%20-Green.pdf* (accessed 16 February 2007).

25. Darrin McMahon, 'Sweep of Reason', *Boston Globe*, 22 June 2003. McMahon noted how Tariq Ali invoked the values of the Enlightenment. Ali's Enlightenment was quite different from that of Thomas Friedman.

26. Steven Weber, an academic at Berkeley, in an interview published at the end of 2002 in California Monthly, quoted by Joan Didion in *Vintage Didion* (New York: Vintage, 2004), p.183.

27. Stephen Bronner, *Reclaiming the Enlightenment* (New York: Columbia University Press, 2004, p.14.

28. Bronner attempts to identify the Enlightenment with a left liberal political programme, and the Counter-Enlightenment with a right-wing conservative programme. This made a certain amount of sense in the 1960s, for example, when social democratic policies coincided with movements for greater social freedom and support for established power coincided with a defence of

'conventional morality'. But the modern right claims the Enlightenment heritage for itself in the shape of neoliberalism's emphasis on personal freedom.

29. David Kelley, 'The Party of Modernity', *Cato Policy Report*, May/June, 2003. vol. xxv, no. 3. In the piece Kelley also argues that the Enlightenment culture was 'an intellectual, not a material or political, phenomenon'. The desire to liberate the Enlightenment from material and political contexts is characteristic of what I call the Folk Enlightenment.

30. Kelley, ibid.

31. Max Boot, 'The case for American Empire', *Weekly Standard*, 15 October 2001.

32. Richard Lowry, 'End Iraq', *National Review*, 15 October 2001.

33. In this context Michael Ledeen famously announced that 'We are the one truly revolutionary country on earth.' It is not clear how sincere the neocons were being, of course, given the deep contempt for democracy and Enlightenment associated with the teachings of Leo Strauss.

34. See Seymour Hersh, 'A case not closed', *New Yorker*, 11 January 1993. In the run-up to the invasion of Iraq, Bush referred to Saddam Hussein as 'the guy who tried to kill my dad' (CNN, 27 September 2002).

35. David Brooks, 'Drafting Hitler', *New York Times*, 9 February 2006.

36. John Lloyd, 'How anti-Americanism betrays the Left', *Observer*, 17 March 2002. Nick Cohen made a similar point in a review of a book by Noam Chomsky published in the *Guardian* on 14 December 2003. Roger Alton and David Aaronovitch also provided liberal, and presumably enlightened, support for the war.

37. Johann Hari, 'Lefties for the war', *Independent*, 25 February 2003.

38. Johann Hari, 'Liberate Iraq now, with or without the UN', *Independent*, 10 January 2003.

39. Hari, op. cit.

40. Norman Geras, 'Apologists amongst us', *Normblog*, 13 July 2005. Similar impulses have led some on the right in Britain to invoke the spirit of Henry Jackson, an American senator, supporter of the New Deal and implacable cold warrior.

41. *The Euston Manifesto*, http://eustonmanifesto.org/joomla/content/view/12/41/.

42. Peter Beinart, 'A fighting faith', *The New Republic*, 13 December 2004. Beinart has developed these ideas at book length.

43. Paul Berman, *Terror and Liberalism* (New York: W. W. Norton, 2003). Berman is at pains to emphasize the importance of irrational mass movements in recent history.

44. Christopher Hitchens, 'The end of Fukuyama', *Slate*, 1 March 2006.

45. Christopher Hitchens, 'Abu Ghraib isn't Guernica', *Slate*, 9 May 2005.

46. Bronner, op. cit. p.6.

47. Karl Popper, *The Open Society and its Enemies*, vol. 2, London: Routledge 2002, Chapter 24, 'The Revolt Against Reason.'

48. I have drawn heavily on Bronner's book in my discussion of postmodernism in Chapter 6.

49. Bronner, op. cit., p.158.

50. Bronner, op. cit, p.146.
51. The Center for Inquiry held a conference in New York entitled 'Toward a new Enlightenment' in October 2005. Speakers included the Nobel Laureates Sir Herman Kroto and Herbert Hauptman, together with Richard Dawkins and Sir Hermann Bondi. The Institute of Ideas in London held an event in the same month called 'Reassessing the Enlightenment for the 21st century'.
52. Recent examples include Lewis Wolpert's *Six Impossible Things Before Breakfast: The Evolutionary Origins of Belief* (London: Faber and Faber, 2006) and Daniel C. Dennett's *Breaking the Spell: Religion as a Natural Phenomenon* (London: Allen Lane, 2006). The key figure in this urgent and enlightened writing about religion is of course the incomparable Richard Dawkins, who has recently waded in with *The God Delusion* (London: Bantam, 2006).
53. See David Kelley's remarks quoted in Walter Olson, 'Dark Bedfellows', *Reason Magazine*, January 1999.
54. Salman Rushdie, 'Defend the right to be offended', *openDemocracy*, 7 February 2005.
55. Francis Wheen, *How Mumbo Jumbo Conquered the World*, (London: Harpercollins 2004), p.8.
56. Wheen, ibid.
57. Wheen, ibid., p.311–12. Wheen does at least notice neoliberal economics in his attack on Counter-Enlightenment, but he is forced to explain the policies of the World Bank and the IMF simply in terms of folly and indifference to evidence. That the neoliberal institutions might be the useful idiots of other interests does not fit into his theoretical model. Doubtless he would consider such an idea to be a conspiracy theory. Whether he would do so regardless of the evidence I cannot say.
58. Polly Toynbee, 'In the name of God', *Guardian*, 22 July 2005.
59. Melanie Phillips 'The flight from reason?' *Daily Mail*, 10 January 2004. She goes on to point out that these beliefs are 'associated with no less a personage than the Prime Minister's wife'. Frank Furedi and Francis Wheen also express concern about Mrs Blair's private beliefs. It is as though they found in her a modern Marie Antoinette and in their eagerness to re-enact the Enlightenment they give themselves over to the hostile resentment of the *tricoteuses*.
60. Dick Taverne, *The March of Unreason* (Oxford: Oxford University Press, 2005), p.4.
61. Taverne, ibid., p.10.
62. Taverne, ibid., p.15.
63. Wheen, op. cit., p.7. '*Trahison des clercs*' means more or less 'the treason of the intellectuals'.
64. Taverne, op. cit., p.3.
65. Frank Furedi, 'The age of unreason', *Spectator*, 19 November 2005.
66. Phillips, op. cit. Phillips writes for the sternly rationalist *Daily Mail* and energetically challenges the scientific consensus on climate change.
67. Kelley, op.cit.
68. See also Cathy Young's article 'The collapse of reason', *Boston Globe*, 29 May 2006.

69. Peter Grier and Faye Bowers, 'Iraq blasts fit pattern of sabotage', *Christian Science Monitor*, 20 August 2003.
70. *Progress Report on the Global War on Terrorism*, September 2003. http://www.whitehouse.gov/home/and/progress/index.html
71. Colin Powell, *Remarks at City College, New York*, 10 November 2003. http://www.state.gov/secretary/former/powell/remarks/2003/26074.htm
72. Quotes come from the Richard Dawkins Foundation website, *http://richard-dawkins.net*. See also Steven Swinford, 'Godless Dawkins challenges schools', *Sunday Times*, 19 November 2006.
73. Harris's ideas are explored in more detail in Chapter 4.
74. Sam Harris, *The End of Faith*, New York: Free Press. There are of course important exceptions to this. Noam Chomsky seems to me to embody the ideal of the enlightened intellectual. But he has never pretended that unreason is the most serious, much less the only, threat to the values of the Enlightenment.
75. Simon Caterson, 'Mumbo-Jumbo and Me,' *The Age*, 15 October 2005.

CHAPTER 2: WHAT WAS ENLIGHTENMENT?

1. Ree is quoted in Madeleine Bunting, 'The convenient myth that changed a set of ideas into western values', *Guardian*, 10 April 2006. See also Roy Porter, *Enlightenment: Britain and the Creation of the Modern World* (London: Allen Lane, 2001), p.4–5.
2. See, for example, Porter, op. cit., p.9. As we saw at the beginning of the book, Locke remains an important figure in the Anglo-American world. See also Kees van der Pijl, 'Lockean Europe?', *New Left Review*, Jan/Feb, 2006, vol. 37.
3. Jonathan Israel, *Radical Enlightenment: Philosophy and the Making of Modernity, 1650–1750* (Oxford: Oxford University Press, 2001).
4. See, for example, John Robertson, *The Case for Enlightenment: Scotland and Naples, 1680–1760* (Cambridge: Cambridge University Press, 2005). I am indebted to Chris Brooke's weblog 'The Virtual Stoa' for this reference. See *http://virtualstoa.net* (accessed 16 February 2007).
5. Porter, op. cit., p.30.
6. From *A Letter Concerning Toleration*, quoted in Isaac Kramnick, *The Portable Enlightenment Reader* (New York: Viking, 1995), p.82. It is also this desire to protect the individual and his property from an activist state that informs the American move towards revolution in the later decades of the eighteenth century. In this respect, the American Revolution is also a reprise of the Glorious Revolution.
7. For a more detailed discussion of the politics of science, see Chapter 5.
8. See, for example, John Gray, *Al Qaeda and What it Means to be Modern* (London: Granta, 2004). In Gray's work the historical Enlightenment's interest in improving the material conditions of mankind is described as a utopian project to transform the human condition. As such its spirit is found in revolutionary communism, Nazism and neoliberalism (ibid., p.44). It is true

that Enlightenment has inspired fanatical reforming zeal – pernicious optimism – but Hume makes it impossible to believe that the Enlightenment was *really* totalitarian.

9. Porter, op. cit., p.20.
10. Peter Gay, *The Enlightenment: An Interpretation* (Harmondsworth: Penguin, 1968), vol. 2, p.137. The suggestion that Voltaire's praise of Newton served a polemical purpose comes from Gay.
11. Porter, op. cit., p.7.
12. Friedrich Nietzsche, *Beyond Good and Evil* (New York: Vintage, 1966), p.191.
13. There are important exceptions to this, of course. Human rights campaigners identify Voltaire as a key figure in their history.
14. Norman Hampson, *The Enlightenment* (Harmondsworth: Penguin, 1968), cited in Roy Porter, *The English Enlightenment* (Harmondsworth: Penguin, 2000), p.3.
15. The frontispiece of Thomas Sprat's *History of the Royal Society* (London, 1667) shows the philosophers crowning a bust of Francis Bacon, for example.
16. Quoted in Hampson, op. cit., p.36.
17. Francis Bacon, *The Proficiency and Advancement of Learning*, quoted in John Henry, *Knowledge is Power* (Cambridge: Icon, 2002), p.54. Henry's book is a superb introduction to Bacon and I have relied on his insights into the role played by magic in this chapter.
18. Francis Bacon, *The New Organon* I, Aphorism 83, quoted in Henry, op. cit., p.143.
19. Stephen Bronner doesn't mention Bacon at all in *Reclaiming the Enlightenment* (New York: Columbia University Press, 2004). Peter Gay's study focuses on the French and doesn't have much to say about the scientific revolution. Porter and Israel differ in almost every respect in their writings about the Enlightenment, but both of them largely ignore Bacon. As we shall see, Theodor W. Adorno and Max Horkheimer's *Dialectic of Enlightenment*, first published in 1944, makes Bacon stand for the Enlightenment as a whole.
20. As a senior lawyer, Bacon was party to the torture of at least two men.
21. Henry, op. cit., p.40.
22. Porter, op. cit., p.2.
23. Isaac Kramnick, *The Portable Enlightenment Reader* (New York: Penguin, 1995), p.1.
24. Kramnick, op. cit. p.2.
25. The modern guardians are all of course friends of the Enlightenment. As they steer us away from 'conspiracy theories' and 'naive utopianism' they encourage us to be fearless inheritors of Voltaire and Locke. 'Be enlightened, of course,' they say, 'only do not think for yourself!'
26. A figure of Frederick's executive excellence could tolerate such a conceit, but Kant's nevertheless presents a serious challenge to all claims to legitimacy that do not rest on universal reason and the approbation of a nation of scholars.
27. Kramnick, op. cit., p.2. Kant should teach us to be more wary than we are of imagining that an enlightened form of government necessarily secures the substantial reality of Enlightenment.

28. Our position within institutions calls for the use of private reason, because we are required to submit to these institutions as a condition of remaining and advancing within them. We are implicated as private individuals who wish to survive and prosper in the world as it is presently constituted. Whereas when we debate as scholars we are disinterested – the public realm of scholarship (distinct from university employment) permits us to use our public reason. I am getting ahead of myself, but Kant here provides a powerful corrective to the very common idea that we can find full, human satisfaction in corporate life. The state and corporate institutions on which most of us depend for our livelihoods cannot permit us to think freely and clearly. They will either deceive us, or demand that we deceive ourselves, if they can. And only a separate and militant public sphere can secure for us a clear understanding of their deceptive nature, and the inadequacy of a life dedicated exclusively to their demands.

29. Kramnick, op. cit., p.3.
30. Kramnick, op. cit., p.6.

CHAPTER 3: THE MENACE IN THE EAST

1. Christopher Hitchens, 'Against rationalization', *The Nation*, 20 September 2001.
2. Sasha Abramsky, 'Our Al Qaeda problem', *The Progressive*, October 2005.
3. Paul Berman, *Terror and Liberalism* (New York: W. W. Norton, 2004), p.xii.
4. Ibid., p.149.
5. Ibid., p.153.
6. Peter Beinart, *The Good Fight* (New York: HarperCollins, 2006). For a more substantial critique of Berman's book, see *http://aaronovitch.blogspot.com*, 15 April, 'Terror and liberalism', 1–7.
7. Martin Amis, 'The age of horrorism', *Observer*, 10 September 2006.
8. Martin Amis, 'You ask the questions', *Independent*, 15 January 2007.
9. For a brief account of the US government's mind control programme, see Alexander Cockburn and Jeffrey St Clair's, *Whiteout: The CIA, Drugs and the Press* (London: Verso, 1998), pp.189–214.
10. 'Zion's Christian soldiers', CBS website, 8 June 2003. Falwell was speaking on *60 Minutes*. Available at http://www.cbsnews.com/stories/2002/10/03/60minutes/main524268.shtml (accessed 16 February 2007).
11. Ken Silverstein and Michael Scherer, 'Born-again Zionists', *Mother Jones*, September/October 2002.
12. CNN Transcript: *http://rtranscripts.cnn.com/TRANSCRIPTS/0603/14/situroom.02.html* (accessed 16 February 2007).
13. Richard T. Cooper, 'General casts war in religious terms', *Los Angeles Times*, 16 October 2003.
14. Paul Wood, 'Fixing the problem of Fallujah', BBC online, 7 November 2004, *http://news.bbc.co.uk/2/hi/middle_east/3989639.stm* (accessed 16 February 2007).

15. NSC-68, 'United States objectives and programs for national security', part IV, 14 April 1950.
16. Richard Stengel, 'Questionable mission to Moscow', *Time*, 24 May 1982. By 1979, Graham had moved away from a hardline Cold War position and by 1982 was being criticized by *Time*, the magazine that had helped launch his career.
17. http://www.etext.org/Politics/Essays/media-monopoly. See also Bagdikian, Ben, *The New Media Monopoly*.
18. Billy Graham website, http://www.billygraham.org/mediaRelations/bios.asp?p=1.
19. Jeanne Kirkpatrick, 'Dictatorships and double standards', *Commentary*, November 1979.
20. Natasha Walter, 'We are just watching as things get worse', *Guardian*, 28 November 2006.
21. Quoted in John Stauber and Sheldon Rampton, *Weapons of Mass Deception* (London: Constable and Robinson, 2003), p.130.
22. In early 2006 the Pentagon started referring to the 'Long War', rather than the War on Terror. Simon Tisdall and Ewen MacAscill, 'America's Long War', *Guardian*, 15 February 2006. See also Austin Bay, 'The Millennium War', *Weekly Standard*, 3 January 2005. Bay suggests that 'Millennium War' captures 'the chronological era and the ideological dimensions of the conflict'. Whether he means that the war started near the turn of the millennium or is going to last a thousand years is not clear.
23. Karen Tumulty, 'It's World War III, says Newt', *Time*, 17 July 2006.
24. Quadrennial Defense Review, Department of Defense (US), 6 February 2006. See also Tisdall and MacAskill, op. cit.
25. See, for example, 'Bush Signs Terror Trial Bill,' 17 October 2006, BBC website. Bush signed into law 'a system of special tribunals' for trying suspected terrorists. http://news.bbc.co.uk/2/hi/americas/6058970.stm.
26. David Brown, 'Study claims Iraq's "Excess deaths toll has reached 655,000"', *Washington Post*, 11 October 2006.
27. 'Gunships attack suspected al Qaeda fighters in Somalia', CNN, 9 January 2007.

CHAPTER 4: FAITH VERSUS REASON

1. Transcript at *http://richarddawkins.net/foundation,ourMission*
2. An mp3 of Sir Henry Kroto's lecture can be found at http://kierenmccarthy.co.uk/2006/06/17/can-the-internet-save-the-enlightenment-the-annual-simonyi-lecture.
3. Sam Harris, *The End of Faith* (New York: The Free Press, 2005), p.15.
4. Harris, op. cit., p.45.
5. Quote from *http://richarddawkins.net/quotes* (accessed 16 February 2007).
6. Harris, op. cit., p.13.
7. Quoted in Norman Hampson, *The Enlightenment* (London: Penguin, 1968), pp.121–2.

8. Reuters, 20 November 2005.
9. Stephen Jay Gould, 'Nonoverlapping magisteria' *Natural History*, March 1997, vol. 106, pp. 16–22.
10. Harris, op. cit., p.224.
11. Harris, op. cit., p.226.
12. The beauty of true statements does incline some people towards Enlightenment – to belief in our duty to truth. But this beauty no more *necessitates* Enlightenment than the beauty of the world *necessitates* belief in a loving God.
13. Quoted in Richard Dawkins, *The God Delusion* (London: Transworld, 2006), p.67.
14. Harris, op. cit., pp.48–9.
15. Harris, op. cit., p.225.
16. Sam Harris, op. cit., p.18. His text uses a slightly different translation, but the gist is the same. Fundamentalists should have executed the President and the First Lady in the summer of 1988 at the very latest; they had been unmasked as sorcerers by a close associate.
17. Leviticus, 18: 9–14, New International Version.
18. Donald Regan, Reagan's former Chief of Staff, made the revelations in a book called *For the Record: From Wall Street to Washington* (New York: Harcourt Brace Jovanovich, 1988).
19. The sheer range of political views considered to be consistent with fundamentalist religion should be a commonplace in all discussions of religion.
20. See Mike Davis, *Planet of Slums* (London: Verso, 2006) for an account of 'slumification' in the South.
21. Barbara Victor, *The Last Crusade* (London: Constable and Robinson, 2005), p.7.
22. Bill Mckibben tells us that 12 per cent of Americans believe Joan of Arc was Noah's wife. Bill McKibben, 'How a faithful nation gets Jesus wrong', *Harpers*, September 2005.
23. 'Which side was God on?', BBC website, http://news.bbc.co.uk/2/hi/americas/6137208.stm
24. Daniel Lazare, 'The gods must be crazy', *Nation*, 28 October 2004.
25. Michael Scanlon, 'Louisiana political budget outline', document dated 23 October 2001, quoted in *'Gimme Five' – Investigation of Tribal Lobbying Matters, Final Report before the Committee on Indian Affairs*, 22 June 2006, p.249.
26. Email to Jack Abramoff, 12 November 2001.
27. See *'Gimme Five'*, op. cit.
28. *'Gimme Five'*, op. cit., p.12.
29. *'Gimme Five'*, op. cit., p.7.
30. Quoted in Roger Kimball, 'The treason of the intellectuals and the undoing of thought', *New Criterion Online*, http://www.newcriterion.com/archive/11/dec92/treason.htm (accessed 16 February 2007).
31. Thomas B. Edsall, 'In Ga., Abramoff scandal threatens a political ascendancy', *Washington Post*, 16 January 2006.
32. John Stauber and Sheldon Rampton, *Banana Republicans* (London: Constable, 2004), p.54.

33. The direct quotations and the information about the FCC rule changes come from *Banana Republicans* (London: Robinson Publishing, 2004) pp.54–5. The authors of that book cite Sara Diamond's *Spiritual Warfare* (Boston, MA: South End Press, 1989) as a source.
34. See, for example, Thomas Franks' *What's the Matter with Kansas?* (New York: Metropolitan Books, 2004) for more on the heart-breaking self-denial of Evangelical voters.
35. Theodor W. Adorno and Max Horkheimer, *The Dialectic of Enlightenment* (London: Verso, 1979), p.20. 'The paradoxical nature of faith degenerates into a swindle, and becomes the myth of the twentieth century; and its irrationality turns it into an instrument of rational administration by the wholly enlightened as they steer society towards barbarism.'
36. This makes a perverse kind of sense in terms of attracting converts. The destruction of the social security system and of middle-class job security provides ideal conditions for expanding the Evangelical churches.
37. George Monbiot, 'Their beliefs are bonkers but they are at the heart of power', *Guardian*, 20 April, 2004.
38. See Joel Bakan, *The Corporation* (London: Constable, 2004), p.35.
39. Supreme Court of Georgia, *Railroad* vs. *Collins*, 1929. Quoted in Ted Nace, *Gangs of America*, (San Francisco: Berrett-Koehler, 2003), p.219.
40. These characteristics come from Dr Robert Hare and are quoted from Bakan, op. cit., pp.56–7.
41. See especially Bakan, op. cit.
42. The description is attributed to Lord Thurlow, an eighteenth-century British lawyer and politician.
43. Dick Taverne, *The March of Unreason* (Oxford: Oxford University Press, 2005), p.224.

CHAPTER 5: THE THREAT TO SCIENCE

1. Cited in Frank Furedi, 'Putting the human back into humanism', *http://www.spiked-online.com*, November 2006.
2. *Spectator*, 19 November 2005.
3. Dick Taverne, *The March of Unreason* (Oxford: Oxford University Press, 2005), p.5.
4. Taverne, op. cit., p.192. Taverne, as is characteristic of a writer in his genre, also worries at length about the threat posed by postmodernism.
5. 'Iceland hypocrisy', *http://www.sirc.org/articles/iceland.html* (accessed 16 February 2007).
6. Taverne, op. cit., p.50. Taverne's scale of priorities is broadly representative of the writings of the Folk Enlightenment. Pharmaceutical corporations employ scientists and their public relations departments to say nice things about science, so they are therefore incapable of being 'anti-science'. Once one has grasped that central organizing insight, the rest of this stuff practically writes itself.
7. Source: OECD, *http://www.oecd.org*.

8. Erzard Ernst, 'Herbal medicines put into context', *Student BMJ*, January 2004. It is fair to say that this figure probably underreports deaths caused by herbal medicines to some extent.
9. Michael Castleman, 'The other drug war', *Mother Jones*, November/December 1998.
10. Marcia Angell, *The Truth about the Drug Companies* (New York: Random House, 2004), pp.104–8.
11. David Healy, *Let Them Eat Prozac* (New York: New York University Press, 2004), p.284.
12. The new generation of antidepressants led to the publication of a number of popular science books and memoirs about depression and the role that drugs could play in its treatment. The genre included Peter D. Kramer's *Listening to Prozac* (New York: Viking Penguin, 1993), Elizabeth Wurtzel's *Prozac Nation* (Boston, MA: Houghton Mifflin, 1994), Lauren Slater's *Prozac Diary* (New York: Random House, 1998) and Andrew Solomon's *Noonday Demon* (New York: Scribner's, 2001).
13. Healy, op. cit., p.265.
14. Ibid., p.266.
15. Ibid., p.266.
16. Ibid., p.132.
17. Dr Gurkirpal Singh, in testimony to the US Senate Finance Committee, 18 November 2004. *http://www.senate.gov/~finance/sitepages/hearing111804.htm* (accessed 17 February 2007). Where no reference is given, other quotations from Dr Singh in this section come from his testimony to the Senate Finance Committee.
18. Ibid.
19. David Graham, testimony to the US Senate Finance Committee, 18 November 2004. *http://www.senate.gov/~finance/sitepages/hearing111804.htm* (accessed 17 February 2007).
20. Rita Rubin, 'How did Vioxx debacle happen?', *USA Today*, 12 October 2004.
21. Dr Gurkirpal Singh, op. cit. Singh was 'strongly in favor' of the cox-2 inhibitors until he learned of the VIGOR results. Yet once he started to ask for more details from the study he was told that his life could be made 'very difficult'.
22. David Graham, interview Manette Loudon, 30 August 2005, *http://www.newstarget.com/011401.html* (accessed 17 February 2007).
23. 'In September 2001 the FDA ordered the company to send doctors a letter "to correct false or misleading impressions and information" about Vioxx's effect on the cardiovascular system', quoted from Rubin, op. cit.; see also Dr Gurkipal Singh, op. cit.
24. Graham, interview with Manette Loudon, op. cit.
25. Rubin, op. cit.
26. In January 2006 the *Guardian* carried a front-page news story about deaths associated with Ritalin. Fifty-one people in the USA had died while on the drug. The news story measured roughly 6 cm by 6 cm. Giving coverage to

Vioxx proportionate to the number of fatalities in both cases would require a front-page news story measuring 60 metres by 60 metres.

27. Graham, testimony to the US Senate Finance Committee, op. cit.
28. Ibid.
29. Ibid.
30. Ibid.
31. Ibid.
32. Ibid.
33. Graham, interview with Manette Loudon, op. cit.
34. Joel Bakan, *The Corporation* (London: Constable, 2004), p.49. The figures come originally from Rachel Cohen of Doctors without Borders.
35. Healy, op. cit., p.123. Folate is the form of folic acid found in leafy vegetables.
36. 'Poor diet linked to bad behaviour', *http://www.bbc.co.uk*, 22 November 2004.
37. Felicity Lawrence, 'Severely troubled boys "soothed by fish oils"', *Guardian*, 12 October 2006.
38. 'Poor diet linked to bad behaviour', op. cit.
39. Bacteria in the stomach might also be a major cause of stomach cancer as well as stomach ulcers.
40. Review by the author, 3 November 2006. Cancer Research UK was unable to provide more detailed information.
41. Yochum is quoted in 'Sunshine "vital to good health"', *Guardian*, 8 June 2004. See also 'Vitamin D "can lower cancer risk"', *http://www.bbc.co.uk*, 28 December 2005, and 'Vitamin D "slashes cancer risk"', *http://www.bbc.co.uk*, 15 September 2006.
42. 'We need to talk: The case for psychological therapy on the NHS', *http://www.mind.org.uk*. See also *http://www.nice.org.uk* (ref: CG023) for their recommendations.
43. Healy, op. cit., p.xiv.
44. Arpad Pusztai's long career as a food safety researcher came to an abrupt end when his work on a type of genetically modified potato indicated a possible threat to human health. He was subject to a vigorous campaign of vilification for alleged shortcomings in his work. Epidemiologist Shiriki Kumanyika came under attack when she co-authored a report for the World Health Organization on diet that recommended limiting 'free sugars' to 10 per cent of daily calories. The academics David Healy and Nancy Olivieri ran into deep trouble when they came into conflict with commercial interests. Healy himself has said that 'several players in the Prozac story were told that it would not be a wise career move for them to raise concerns about Prozac' (Healy, op. cit., p.125). Remarks made by Dr Singh, quoted above, suggest that similar pressure was brought to bear in the Vioxx case.
45. 'Drug company pulls funding after conference criticism', *PR Watch*, 10 November 2006 – *http://www.prwatch.org/node/5461* (accessed 17 February 2007).
46. *http://www.acsh.org/about* (accessed 17 February 2007).
47. Edwin Feulner, President of the Heritage Foundation, quoted on the ACSH website, *http://www.acsh.org/about* (accessed 17 February 2007).

48. Gilbert Ross, 'Don't kill the pharmaceutical golden goose: Tort litigation against Merck can destroy new drugs – and lives', 18 November 2004, available online at *http://www.acsh.org/news/newsID.1000/news_detail.asp* (accessed 17 February 2007).

49. Quotes come from 'Consultation Report', Science Media Centre, March 2002, available online at *http://www.sciencemediacentre.org/consultation.htm* (accessed 17 February 2007). As a summary of attitudes in the scientific establishment the report speaks with unintentional eloquence of the ability of power to make itself inaccessible to thought.

50. Anniversary address at the Royal Society, 2005. See *http://www.royalsoc.ac.uk/publication.asp?year=2005&id=2181* for the text of Lord May's speech (accessed 17 February 2007).

51. I have not described the efforts by corporations to promote doubt about the dangers of tobacco, global warming and a diet high in hydrogenated fats and refined sugar. Together these campaigns constitute an extremely serious threat to reason.

CHAPTER 6: POSTMODERNISM AND THE ASSAULT ON TRUTH

1. Ophelia Benson and Jeremy Strangroom, *Why Truth Matters* (London: Continuum, 2006), p.18.

2. Frank Furedi, *Where Have All the Intellectuals Gone?* (London: Continuum, 2004), p.4.

3. Ibid, p.46.

4. Richard Wolin, *The Seduction of Unreason* (Princeton: Princeton University Press, 2004), pp.312–13.

5. Alan Sokal, a physicist, persuaded a cultural studies journal, *Social Text*, to publish a mishmash of nonsense under this title.

6. Alan Sokal and Jean Bricmont, *Intellectual Impostures* (London: Profile, 1998), quoted in Raymond Tallis, 'Sokal and Bricmont: Is this the beginning of the end of the dark ages in the humanities?', *PN Review*, June 1999, no.128.

7. The Americans interfered in Latin America because the 'unenlightened' in those countries could not be trusted with self-rule. See, for example, Chris Carlson, 'Washington and its contempt for Venezuela', *Znet*, January 2007.

8. 'M'Kinley memorial services at Albany', *New York Times*, 15 March 1902. The words were spoken by former Postmaster General Charles Emory Smith.

9. This phrase was originally coined by Jean-Francis Lyotard. A metanarrative in this context is an account of the world that seeks to ascribe some overarching meaning or significance to human history.

10. Quoted in Theodor W. Adorno and Max Horkheimer, *Dialectic of Enlightenment* (London: Verso, 1997), pp.3–4.

11. Ibid., p.4.

12. Ibid., p.6.

13. Ibid., p.xvi.
14. Ibid., p.42.
15. Stephen Bronner, *Reclaiming the Enlightenment* (New York: Columbia University Press, 2004), p.116.
16. Ibid., p.114. Bronner is quoting Thomas Mann. Ironically the strategy outlined here is particularly widespread among employees of the 'culture industry'.
17. Anthony Lewis, 'If NAFTA loses', *New York Times*, 5 November 1993, quoted in the notes to Noam Chomsky's *Understanding Power* (2002), compiled by Peter R. Mitchell and John Schoeffel – *http://www.understandingpower.com/chap8.htm* (accessed 17 February 2007).
18. Sandra Polaski, 'NAFTA at year 12', oral testimony to the United States Senate Subcommittee on International Trade of the Committee on Finance, 11 September 2006. Available online at *http://www.carnegieendowment.org/files/naftaoraltestimony.pdf* (accessed 17 February 2006).
19. Joel Bakan, *The Corporation* (London: Constable, 2004), p.93.
20. Charles Dilke, *Greater Britain: A Record of Travel in the English-Speaking Countries*, 8th edn (London: Macmillan, 1885), p.217.
21. Ibid., p.564.
22. Ibid., p.85.
23. Ibid.
24. David Morgan, 'Yale study: US eugenics paralleled Nazi Germany', *Chicago Tribune*, 15 February 2000. Available online at *http://www.commondreams.org/headlines/021500–02.htm* (accessed 17 February 2007).
25. 'Anthropology and counterinsurgency: the strange story of their curious relationship', *Military Review*, March/April 2005, quoted in *Lobster*, Winter 2005/2006, vol. 50. The author notes that the move away from 'descriptive ethnography' after Vietnam has left it 'conspicuously absent as a discipline within our national-security enterprise' – an absence that has created problems for the conduct of counter-insurgency warfare in Iraq.
26. Bronner, op. cit., p.99.
27. Taking advantage of the opportunity created by anthropology's retirement from government work, perhaps.
28. Anne Hendrixson, 'Angry young men, veiled young women: Constructing a new population threat', Briefing 34, The Corner House, December 2004, drawing on G. E. Fuller and R. Hoch, 'Youth bulges in Asia', 1998, 'unpublished article on file with the author'. The Corner House Report also cites a nerve-wracking article in *International Security* called 'A surplus of men, a deficit of peace' (Spring 2002) which suggests dealing with problems of the 'youth bulge' by fighting surplus young men encouraging their self-destruction, or exporting them. Scientific inquiry still risks collapsing into eliminationist fantasy.
29. Ibid.
30. Peter Schwart and Doug Randall, 'An Abrupt Climate Change Scenario, and its Implications for United States Security', October 2003, available online at http://www.environmentaldefense.org/documents/3566_AbruptClimate-Change.pdf

CHAPTER 7: AN ACTUALLY EXISTING INFAMY

1. On some reckonings, the US state even contains the UK state, at least in its defence and security functions. Sir Timothy Garden, Former Assistant Chief of the Defence Staff, has said that to describe the MOD as 'operating as a wholly owned subsidiary of the Pentagon' would be 'slightly extreme' but 'probably about right' (*File on 4*, 28 January 2003). A representative from the CIA attends meetings of Britain's Joint Intelligence Committee.
2. Remarks made by Donald Rumsfeld, 10 September 2001. Available online at *http://www.defenselink.mil/speeches/2001/s20010910-secdef.html* (accessed 20 February 2007).
3. 'The war on waste', CBS website, 29 January 2002. http://www.cbsnews.com/stories/2002/01/29/eveningnews/main325985.shtml
4. Paul Berman, *Terror and Liberalism*, (New York: W. W. Norton, 2004), p.xii.
5. Daniel Ellsberg, *Secrets: A Memoir of Vietnam and the Pentagon Papers* (New York: Penguin, 2000), p. 43.
6. Daniel Ellsberg, op. cit., Ellsberg's book provides a remarkable insight into the operations of the US state in the 1960s.
7. Quoted in Richard J. Aldritch, *The Hidden Hand* (London: John Murray, 2001), p. 638.
8. 'Fooling America', a talk by Robert Parry given in Santa Monica, California, 28 March 1993.
9. See, for example, 'Wolfowitz's comments revive doubts over Iraq's WMDs', USA Today Online, 30 May 2003. Available at *http://www.usatoday.com/news/world/iraq/2003-05-30-wolfowitz-iraq_x.htm* (accessed 20 February 2007).
10. 'Top Bush officials push case against Saddam', CNN Online, 8 September 2002. Available at *http://archives.cnn.com/2002/ALLPOLITICS/09/08/iraq.debate/* (accessed 20 February 2007).
11. Speech in Ohio, October 2002. Transcript available online at *http://www.narsil.org/war_on_iraq/bush_october_7_2002.html* (accessed 20 February 2007).
12. Cited in David Miller, 'Information Dominance', *http://www.coldtype.net/Assets.04/Essays.04/Miller.pdf*. The Joint Vision document is at *http://www.dtic.mil/jointvision/jvpub2.htm*. (Accessed 20 February 2007.)
13. Quoted in Miller, op. cit. Also online at *http://www.iwar.org.uk/iwar/resources/info-dominance/issue-paper.htm* (accessed 20 February 2007).
14. Committee to Protect Journalists, cited in Sherry Ricciardi, 'Dangerous assignment', *American Journalism Review*, December/January 2006.
15. Miller, op. cit., p.9. Miller cites Phillip, Knightley, 'History or bunkum' in David Miller (ed.), *Tell Me Lies: Propaganda and Media Distortion in the Attack on Iraq* (London: Pluto, 2004).
16. 'Al-Jazeera "hit by missile"', 8 April 2003, BBC Online. Available at *http://news.bbc.co.uk/1/hi/world/middle_east/2927527.stm* (accessed 20 February 2007).
17. Quoted in Jeremy Scahill, 'The War on Al Jazeera', *The Nation*, 19 December 2005.

18. Kevin Maguire and Andy Lines, 'Bush plot to bomb his Arab ally', *Daily Mirror*, 22 November 2005. Sources quoted in the article said that 'Bush was deadly serious, as was Blair. That much is absolutely clear from the language used by both men.'

19. 'Hollywood enlists in Bush's war drive', David Walsh, World Socialist Web Site, 19 November 2001, *http://www.wsws.org/articles/2001/nov2001/holl-n19.shtml* (accessed 20 February 2007).

20. J. Hoberman, 'All as it had been', *Village Voice*, 11 December 2001.

21. Alex Constantine, 'Collateral brain damage? The Hollywood propaganda ministry', available online at *http://www.ratical.org/ratville/JFK/JohnJudge/linkscopy/CBD.html* (accessed 20 February 2007).

22. 'Full Spectrum Warrior hits its target', BBC Online, 2 July 2004, at *http://news.bbc.co.uk/1/hi/technology/3855769.stm* (accessed 20 February 2007).

23. ' "America's Army" video game adds real soldiers as characters', Fox News Online, at *http://www.foxnews.com/story/0,2933,213825,00.html* (accessed 20 February 2007).

24. *http://www.sourcewatch.org/index.php?title=America's_Army* has more information about the Pentagon's 'propagaming'. Footage of the Frag Dolls in action can be found at the *America's Army* website: *http://www.americasarmy.com/gallery/videos/AA_SEG_FRAG_DOLLS.mov* (accessed 20 February 2007).

25. *Church Committee Reports*, Book I, 'Foreign and Military Intelligence', Section X.b, 'Covert Relationships with US Media', pp.192–3. Available online at *http://www.aarclibrary.org/publib/church/reports/contents.htm* (accessed 20 February 2007).

26. Ibid.

27. Ibid.

28. Frances Stonor Sanders, *Who Paid the Piper: The CIA and the Cultural Cold War* (London: Granta, 1999), pp.244–51.

29. CIA document, #1035–960. The document also stresses the need for tact: 'We do not recommend that discussion of the assassination question be initiated where it is not already taking place.' Available online at *http://www.webcom.com/~lpease/collections/assassinations/jfk/cia-inst.htm* (accessed 20 February 2007).

30. Joel Bakan, *The Corporation* (New York: Free Press, 2004), p.34.

31. In an interview in 2006, Harold Burson, one of the founders of PR firm Burson-Marsteller, acknowledged Edward Bernays' central role in creating the modern PR industry: 'Bernays thought that he could control public opinion. His methodology, of course, was fundamental. Most of the things we do today were identified by Bernays 80 years ago. He had brilliant ideas. I met him a few times, but didn't like him. He was one of the most egocentric people I have ever met.' Burson-Marsteller is the world's fifth-largest PR company. Available online at *http://www.sourcewatch.org/index.php?title=Harold_Burson_Interviewed_By_Der_Spiegel* (accessed 20 February 2007).

32. John Stauber and Sheldon Rampton, *Toxic Sludge is Good for You* (London: Constable, 2004), p.23.

33. Edward Bernays, *Propaganda* (New York: Ig Publishing, 2005), p.72.

34. Ibid., p.81.
35. Ibid., pp.73–4.
36. Stauber and Rampton, op. cit., p.24.
37. Plato, *The Republic* (London: Penguin, 1987), p.180. The true beliefs of neoconservatives, like those of the Allawi in Syria, are of course a secret, but it is a fair guess that they subscribe to some version of Plato's number nonsense. For an invocation of Greece and Rome to justify limits on democracy, see, for example, Michel Crozier, Samuel Huntington and Joji Watanuki's *The Crisis of Democracy* (New York: Columbia University Press, 1975), p.113 and following.
38. Stauber and Rampton, op. cit., p.23.
39. Richard W. Pollay, 'Propaganda, puffing and the public interest', *Public Relations Review*, Fall 1990, vol. XVI, no. 3. See also Sourcewatch entries on Ivy Lee and Edward Bernays *http://www.sourcewatch.org/index.php?title= Ivy-Lee http://www.sourcewatch.org/index.php?title=Edward-Bernays*
40. Union of Concerned Scientists, *Smoke Mirrors and Hot Air*, January 2007. Available online at *http://www.ucsusa.org/news/press_release/ExxonMobil-GlobalWarming-tobacco.html* (accessed 20 February 2007).
41. For an account of this network of think tanks, see, for example, John Stauber and Sheldon Rampton, *Banana Republicans* (London: Constable and Robinson, 2004), pp.17–46.
42. Bernays, op. cit., p.54.
43. William Schneider, 'Marketing Iraq: Why now?', CNN Online, 12 September 2002. Available at *http://archives.cnn.com/2002/ALLPOLITICS/09/12/schneider.iraq/* (accessed 20 February 2007).
44. Martha Brant, 'Ladies and gentlemen . . . the band', *Newsweek*, 18 September 2002.
45. John Stauber and Sheldon Rampton, 'Risky business: The world according to Hill and Knowlton', *PR Watch*, First Quarter 1997, vol. 4, no. 1.
46. Source: ZenithOptimedia.
47. Jeffrey Faux, *Global Class War* (Chichester: Wylie, 2006), p.160.
48. Alan Rusbridger, *Press Gazette*, 8 September 2005.
49. Edward Herman and Noam Chomsky, *Manufacturing Consent* (New York: Random House, 1988), p.xi.
50. Ibid., p.2.
51. Ben Bagdikian, *The New Media Monopoly* (Boston, MA: Beacon Press, 2004).
52. As I write, serious problems in the global economy are again being cheerfully ignored by the mainstream media.
53. Ken Silverstein, quoted in Michael Massing, 'The end of news?', *New York Review of Books*, 16 December 2005.
54. See Scott Ritter and William Rivers Pitt, *War on Iraq* (London: Profile, 2002). In the months before the invasion of Iraq there were plenty of people who could have cast doubt on official claims about the Iraqi WMD programme. The media largely ignored them.
55. Alongside scientific materialism, neoconservatism and fundamentalist Christianity, we find in the US-UK state a persistent interest in Eastern religion and flat-out occultism.

CHAPTER 8: AN ENLIGHTENED MODEL

1. Michel Foucault, *Power*, (New York: The New Press, 2000), p.133.
2. Plato, *Republic* (London: Penguin, 1987), p.85. It is useful to compare Plato with Irving Kristol in this context (see introduction, note 4).
3. Berman, Morris, *The Twilight of American Culture* (New York: W. W. Norton, 2000).
4. Ibid., p.140.
5. Ibid., p.176.
6. Curtis White, *The Middle Mind* (London: Allen Lane, 2004), p.201.
7. Isaac Kramnick, *The Portable Enlightenment Reader* (New York: Penguin, 1995), p.3.
8. Many political activists already have to negotiate the division between the public and the private that Kant saw as the central organizing dichotomy of Enlightenment.
9. Frank Furedi, *Where Have All the Intellectuals Gone: Confronting 21st Century Philistinism* (London: Continuum, 2004), p.156.
10. Francis Bacon, quoted in Norman Hampson, *The Enlightenment* (London: Penguin, 1968), p.36.
11. For more information about the GPL, see *http://www.gnu.org/copyleft/gpl.html* (accessed 20 February 2007).
12. For more on the history of free software, see Glyn Moody, *Rebel Code* (London: Allen Lane, 2001).
13. The site focuses on the public relations business. Doctors, lawyers, journalists and other professionals might want to think about how similar sites might form the basis for programmes of inquiry into other matters of pressing concern.

CONCLUSION

1. Roy Porter, *Enlightenment: Britain and the Creation of the Modern World* (London: Allen Lane, 2001), pp.483–4.
2. Nerve-wracking subjects that cannot be ignored under conditions of Enlightenment include state and corporate mind-control programmes (see, for example, Dominic Streatfield, *Brainwash: The Secret History of Mind Control* (London: Hodder and Stoughton, 2006)) and fluoridation (see Christopher Bryson, *The Fluoride Deception* (New York: Seven Stories, 2004)). Serious inquiry into the world is likely to make most of us sound like foaming lunatics for considerable periods of time.

Index